WHY INVESTORS FAIL

"Risk comes from not knowing what you're doing."

– Warren Buffett

Vivek Choudhary

To My Hero

Warren Buffett & Howard Homan Buffett

About the Author

Vivek Choudhary is a Value Investor & Entrepreneur who has over 20 years of experience in investment and entrepreneurship. Involve in diversify business Commodities, Manufacturing, Hotel & Automobiles.

He earned MBA in finance & Marketing at IIPM, MDP in Strategic Market Planning at IIM, Equity Research Analyst at BSE Institute, Value Investing at Stanford University Continue studies, and Entrepreneurship Essential & Leading with Finance at HBX Harvard Business School & Value Investing at Columbia Business School, Business Lesson Cohort at Harvard Business School Online.

He is passionate about Value Investing and invests globally. His hobby is reading. Every day he read value investing books and finance books.

He admires his Hero Mr. Warren Buffett Chief Executive Officer of Berkshire Hathaway – He follows his footprint of Value Investing. For him reading and studying are like compounding, it will help him in achieving his passion.

He wrote the book

- **Value Investing & Behavioral Finance**

- **Wealth Creation & Financial Statement Analysis "Dream to be Wealthy"**

- **Value Investing - Legendary Graham & Dodd Valuation**

- **Value Investing CHECKLIST**

- **Billionaires Mind – Blue Print of Entrepreneurship**

- **Why Investors Fail –Mistakes Value Investors Avoid**

www.security-analysis.com

CONTENTS

Preface	VI
Introduction	VII

MISTAKES VALUE INVESTORS AVOID

1. Due Diligence	2
2. Investor or Trader	25
3. Competitive Industry	42
4. Macro Analysis	57
5. Mediocre Business	71
6. Timing The Market	92
7. High Debt	105
8. Forecast	119
9. Corporate Governance	132
10. Financial Distress	152
11. Valuation	163
12. Buffett FAQ	174

PREFACE

"It's good to learn from your mistakes. It's better to learn from other people's mistakes."
— Warren Buffett

What I have learned in value investing is to avoid mistakes, the more I learn, the more I earn, investing does not require to be very intelligent, one needs to be smart and discipline towards investing, there are thousand companies listed and it very hard to understand all of them, it is better to understand few companies and avoid the mistake in investing.

All I Want to Know is Where I'm Going to Die So I'll Never Go There" by Charlie Munger, I keep this in my mind while I selecting a stock, it is better to know what are the mistakes in investing and avoid those mistakes, we can make a very good return from our investment, Every investor tries to learn what has worked in investing and ignore the facts that what has not worked in investing if we know the mistakes in investing, it will help in selecting the right stock. We don't need to do mistakes in our life to learn how an investment works, in this way we can never able to create wealth. I have shared the mistakes investor makes in selecting the stock and value investor avoids those mistakes.

INTRODUCTION

"It is remarkable how much long-term advantage people like us have gotten by trying to be consistently not stupid, instead of trying to be very intelligent."

"Invert, always invert: Turn a situation or problem upside down. Look at it backward. What happens if all our plans go wrong? Where don't we want to go, and how do you get there? Instead of looking for success, make a list of how to fail instead–through sloth, envy, resentment, self-pity, entitlement, all the mental habits of self-defeat. Avoid these qualities and you will succeed. Tell me where I'm going to die so I don't go there."
--Charlie Munger

Warren Buffett knows that what doesn't work in investing, we should be using the same principle in our investment.

In this book, you will be learning, what has not worked in investing and the mistakes investor makes and value investor avoid, you don't have to do all mistakes with all your money, all you need to search for what has not worked in investing and what are you doing currently, that is not been working, you will get all the answer in this books.

Mistakes Investors makes:-

- Due Diligence – they never able to answer this question, why they are buying this company? How company work?
- Investor or Trader – Many people really don't know, who are they? What distinguish them from trader to investor?
- Competitive Industry -Most of the investor never figures it out about the industry competitions and they invest in the poor and highly competitive industry those results in poor return or a negative return.
- Macro Analysis - Many of Investor try to predict the market, what will be interest rate, what will be GDP etc and they fail to understand the MICRO analysis of the company, if you are look at the MACRO factor in your investment and ignore the MICRO factor, you may end up with not making any money.
- Mediocre Business - Ninety-five percent of startups fail within five years. The pain of business failure can be awful; but there is another pain that affects many businesses: the pain of business mediocrity.
- Timing The Market - Market timing is the strategy of making buying or selling decisions of financial assets (often stocks) by attempting to predict future market price movements, that's never work but still investor love to do and burn cash .

- High Debt - When you invest in a company, you need to look at many different financial records to see if it is a worthwhile investment.
- Forecast- Wall Street is the place where investor only forecast, what will be the earning? What will be the free cashflow? What will be price of the stock after six month? Biggest mistakes.
- Corporate governance- is the system of rules, practices, and processes by which a firm is directed and controlled.
- Financial Distress - Many investors not look for quality income state and balance sheet and cash flow, they buy the stock only hope that the price will raise, and it never happen.
- Valuation - Many investor do a valuation by using Discounted Cash Flow as what they have learn in the B school , but value investor , even warren buffet has never used DCF.
- Buffett FAQ – Learn from Warren Buffett that's work in investing.

This Book has all the mistakes investors make, continues making every day without understanding, what will be the result, it could be someone new in investing world or someone is old, till date, you must have learned what works in investing in your B-School or somewhere else, in this book you will read the mistakes and surprising facts of value investing. Value Investors know it very well that what doesn't work and they will never try to do those mistakes. If you will do those mistakes then when you will make money?

So let start learning about mistakes and avoid those mistakes and become successful Value investor.

Q&A –Warren Buffett

Investors eventually repeat their mistakes. How can you prevent this--through fast growth or safety?

- Source: BRK Annual Meeting 1997
- Time: 1997

If you understood a business perfectly and the future of the business, you would need very little in the way of a margin of safety. So, the more vulnerable the business is, assuming you still want to invest in it, the larger margin of safety you'd need. If you're driving a truck across a bridge that says it holds 10,000 pounds and you've got a 9,800 pound vehicle, if the bridge is 6 inches above the crevice it covers, you may feel okay, but if it's over the Grand Canyon, you may feel you want a little larger margin of safety in terms of driving only drive a 4,000 pound truck across. It depends on the nature of the underlying risk. We don't get the margin of safety now that we got in the 1970s.

The best thing is to learn from other guys' mistakes. Patton used to say, "It's an honor to die for your country; make sure the other guy gets the honor." There are a lot of mistakes that I've repeated. The biggest one, the biggest category over time, is being reluctant to pay up a little for a business that I knew was really outstanding. The cost of that I think is in the billions, and I'll probably keep making that mistake. The mistakes are made when there are businesses you can understand and that are attractive and you don't do something about them. I don't worry at all about the mistakes that come about like when I met Bill Gates and didn't buy Microsoft or something like that. Most of our mistakes have been mistakes of omission rather than commission.

MISTAKES VALUE INVESTORS AVOID

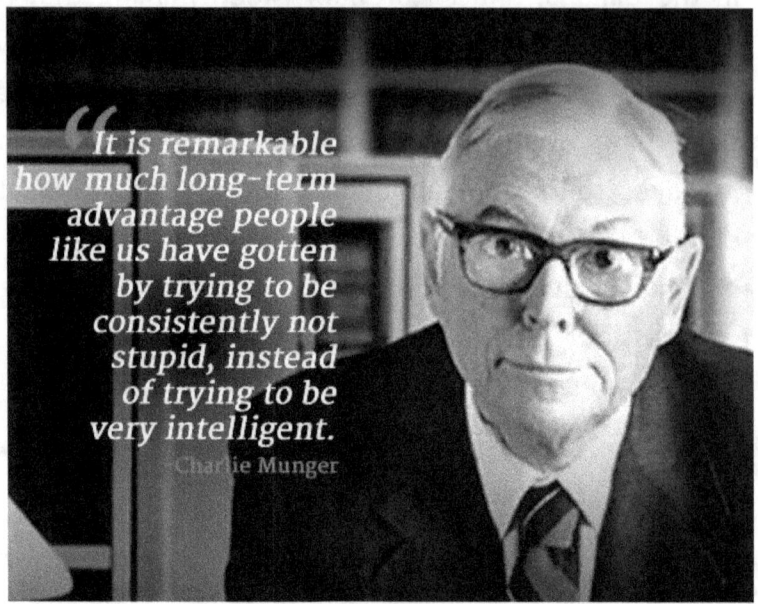

> It is remarkable how much long-term advantage people like us have gotten by trying to be consistently not stupid, instead of trying to be very intelligent.
> —Charlie Munger

OVER **90%** of retail traders lose their capital in 6 months

1

Due Diligence

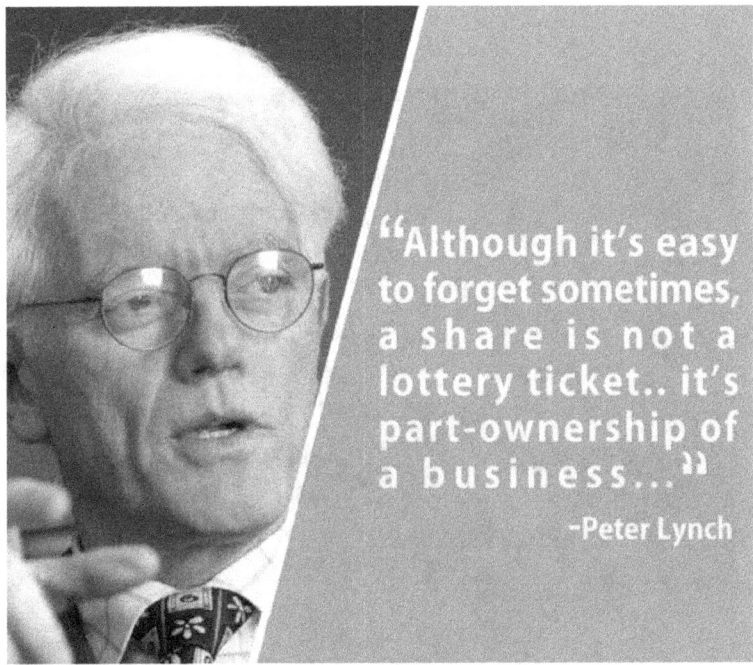

"Although it's easy to forget sometimes, a share is not a lottery ticket.. it's part-ownership of a business..."
-Peter Lynch

Many investors fail to understand that definition of the stock market, many believe it is a place to buy a ticker symbol or a lottery ticket that will make him rich, and they fail several times and never make money.

Too often though, people blindly follow these recommendations or advice without researching themselves. I know reading a stock or fund prospectus can make your eyes glaze over, but they aren't too hard once you know what to look for. Many of these "recommendations" might be paid for by the company who's stock or fund it is. And other recommendations might be based on that person's own goals, but you and your investing situation is unique, you must do your own due diligence before dropping cash.

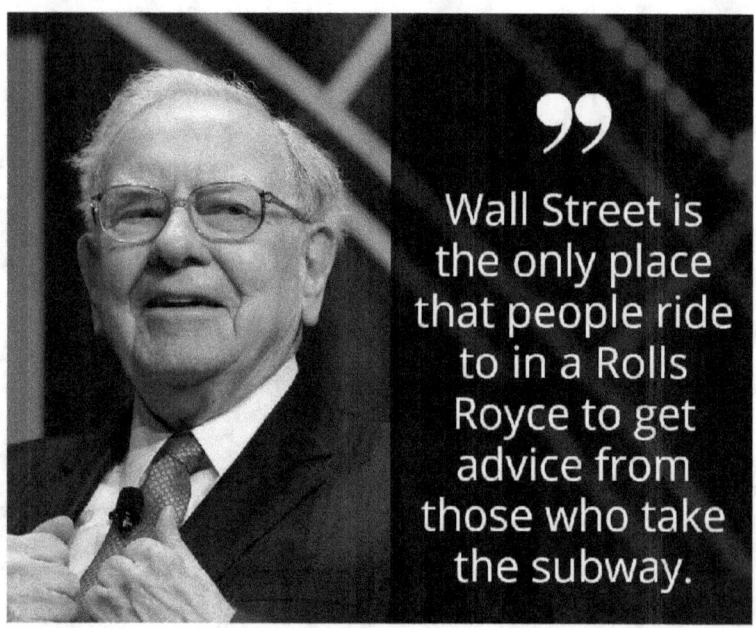

> Wall Street is the only place that people ride to in a Rolls Royce to get advice from those who take the subway.

You are putting your hard-earned money to work, so you must understand the "why" and "what" before investing in something.

Winners & Losers in the Stock Market

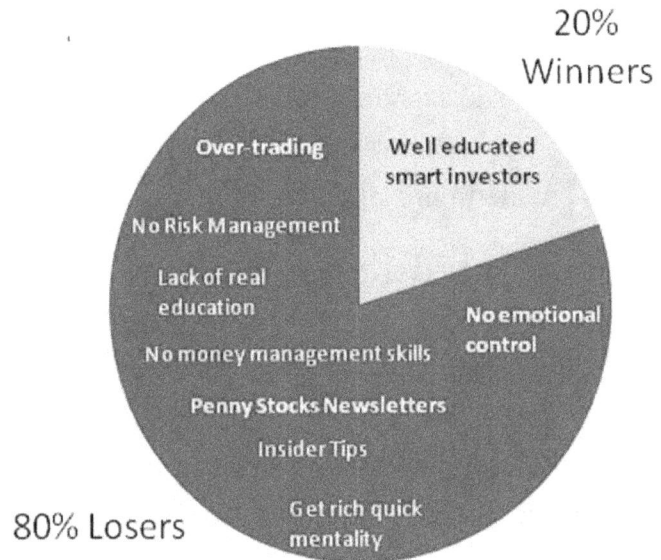

The stock market refers to the collection of markets and exchanges where regular activities of buying, selling, and issuance of shares of publicly-held companies take place. Such financial activities are conducted through institutionalized formal exchanges or over-the-counter (OTC) marketplaces which operate under a defined set of regulations. There can be multiple stock trading venues in a country or a region which allow transactions in stocks and other forms of securities.

A company needs a marketplace where these shares can be sold. This marketplace is provided by the stock market. If everything goes as per the plans, the company will successfully sell the 5 million shares at a price of $10 per share and collect $50 million worth of funds. Investors will get the company shares which they can expect to hold for their preferred duration, in anticipation of rising in share price and any potential income in the form of dividend payments. The stock exchange acts as a facilitator for this capital raising process and receives a fee for its services from the company and its financial partners.

The stock market serves two very important purposes. The first is to provide capital to companies that they can use to fund and expand their businesses. If a company issues one million shares of stock that initially sell for $10 a share, then that provides the company with $10 million of capital that it can use to grow its business (minus whatever fees the company pays for an investment bank to manage the stock offering). By offering stock shares instead of borrowing the capital needed for expansion, the company avoids incurring debt and paying interest charges on that debt.

The secondary purpose the stock market serves is to give investors – those who purchase stocks – the opportunity to share in the profits of publicly-traded companies. Investors can profit from stock buying in one of two ways. Some stocks pay regular dividends (a given amount of money per share of stock someone owns). The other way investors can profit from buying stocks is by selling their stock for a profit if the stock price increases from their purchase price. For example, if an investor buys shares of a company's stock at $10 a share and the price of the stock subsequently raises to $15 a share, the investor can then realize a 50% profit on their investment by selling their shares.

In the short term, price of a stock is guided by demand and supply forces of the market. A stock with great news will have high demand and will see huge buying because people expect it to go up. In the long term, it is the performance of the business that determines the performance of a stock. A business that makes good profits while keeping its expenses low over a long time is a great business to invest in. Serious investors look at great businesses to invest, and stay with it for a long time.

To be a successful investor, it is not enough to buy a stock and hold it. An investor must gain knowledge about the business behind the stock, what it does and how does it make money for itself and its shareholders. Knowing this will not only help understand the business, it will also help in measuring, at least with some certainty, what possibilities the business holds for the future and where it will be after many years. In short, never overlook the business behind the stock as it is the foundation of your long term investment.

Stock market is a great place to make a fortune, but some inexperienced investors look at it as a get rich quick scheme where lot of money can be made in a very short time. Easy access to internet and emergence of discount brokers has made it easy to buy and sell a stock by just clicking a button. This ease of buying and selling has given a reason to treat stocks like lottery tickets. After all why would you keep a stock for ten years, when it can be bought and sold within minutes.

The problem with this style of investing is that it makes little profit for you each time, a rise of half a percent in a stock and we are ready to book profits.

Secondly, frequent buying and selling costs a lot as for every buy and sell, you give a commission to your broker, irrespective of whether you make any money or not. This takes a big chunk of your profit away from you, in the hands of your broker, making him richer while you keep struggling to make money.

Thirdly, short term investing is not very tax friendly, if you invest for less than a year, you attract short term capital gains tax on your profits. On the other hand if you stay invested for at least one year, you don't have to pay any tax.

A sensible investor must look at stocks as a part ownership in a business and not as a lottery ticket. When you invest in a great business for long term, you are actually riding its long term success by being a part owner of it.

Owning a stock that has been doing great for the past few years is just one side of the coin. What an investor must ensure is if the business will be able to sustain, or even improve its business in the future. ? This is what Peter Lynch calls knowing your investments. The second part is finding reasons to own an investment. We own a stock because we expect it to do well in the future, so pull out a paper, and fill it with the reasons why you would like to hold this stock for a long term. If you have a page full of logical reasons to hold, you know you have made a good investment.

It is not enough to know what you own, a sensible and logical investor finds reasons to hold an investment, writing pros and cons of a business, and being rational while making an investment decision is the right path to successful investing.

"*Investing without research is like playing stud poker and never looking at the cards."*
-Peter Lynch

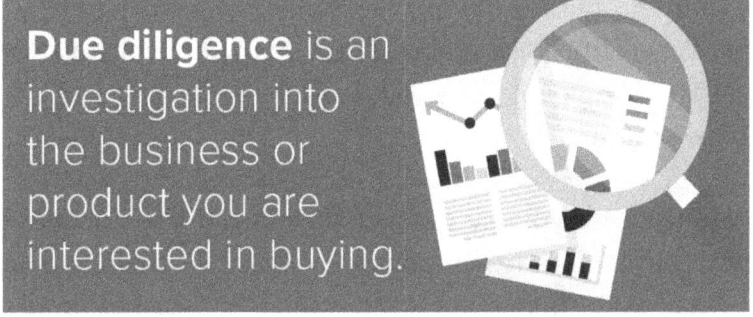

Due diligence is defined as an investigation of a potential investment (such as a stock) or product to confirm all facts. These facts can include such items as reviewing all financial records, past company performance, plus anything else deemed material. For individual investors, doing due diligence on a potential stock investment is voluntary, but recommended.

In the 2008 shareholder meeting of Berkshire Hathaway, a shareholder asked Warren Buffett and Charlie Munger –

"If you could not talk with management, could not read the annual report, and did not know the stock price of the company, but were only allowed to look at its financial statements, what metric would you look at to help you determine whether you should buy the company?"

They replied –

Buffett: Well, what we're doing in investment – and what everybody does – is we're laying out money now to get more money back later on.

Now, let's leave the market aspect of the asset out of it. When you buy a farm, you really aren't thinking about what the market on it is going to be tomorrow, next week, or next month. You're thinking about how many bushels of beans or corn per acre you can get, and what the price is likely to be. You're looking to the asset itself.

And in the case you lay out, the first question you have to ask is, do I understand enough about thus business so that the financial statements can tell me the information that is useful to me to make a judgement about what the future financial statements are going to look like? And in a great majority of cases, the answer would probably be no.

But I've bought stocks the way you're describing many times. And they were in businesses that I thought I understood where if I knew enough about the financial past; it would tell me enough about the financial future that I could buy. Now, I couldn't say the stock was worth X or 105% of X or 95% of X. But if I could buy it at 40% of X, I would feel that I had this margin of safety that Graham talked about, and I could make a decision.

Most times, I wouldn't be able to make it. If you hand me a bunch of financial statements and don't tell me what the business is, there's no way I can make a judgement as to what's going to happen.

So unless I know the nature of business, the financial statements aren't going to tell me much. But if I knew something about the business – or the product – and I just see the financial statements, I may be able to make that judgement.

But we've bought lots and lots of securities – and in the majority of the securities Charlie and I have bought, we've never met or talked to management. We've primarily worked off financial statements, our general understanding of the business, and the specific understanding the industry and the business we're buying. Charlie?

Munger: I think there's one metric we use that others should use more. We tend to prefer the business that makes so much money, that it drowns in cash. One of the main reasons for owning it is you has all of this cash coming in.

Buffett: It's a lot easier to understand a business that's bringing you a check every month…But I bought a lot of things off of financial statements. And there are a lot of things that I wouldn't buy if I knew the management was the most wonderful in the world – because if there in the wrong business, it really doesn't make much difference how good the management is.

The steps are organized so that with each new piece of information, you'll build upon what you previously learned.

In the end, by following these steps, you'll gain a balanced view of the pros and cons of your investment idea. This will allow you to make a rational, logical investment decision.

Company Capitalization

The first step is for you to form a mental picture or diagram of the company you're researching. This is why you'll want to look at the company's market capitalization, which shows you just how big the company is by calculating the total dollar market value of its outstanding shares.

The market capitalization says a lot about how volatile the stock is likely to be, how broad the ownership might be, and the potential size of the company's end markets. For example, large-cap and mega-cap companies tend to have more stable revenue streams and less volatility. Mid-cap and small-cap companies, meanwhile, may only serve single areas of the market and may have more fluctuations in their stock price and earnings.

Revenue, Margin Trends

When you begin looking at the financial numbers related to the company you're researching, it may be best to start with the revenue, profit, and margin trends. Look up the revenue and net income trends for the past two years.

You should also review profit margins to see if they are generally rising, falling, or remaining the same. You can find specific information regarding profit margins by going directly to the company's website and searching their investor relations section for their quarterly and annual financial statements.

Competitors and Industries

Now that you have a feel for how big the company is and how much money it earns, it's time to size up the industries it operates in and who it competes with. Compare the margins of two or three competitors. Every company is partially defined by who it competes with. Just by looking at the major competitors in each line of the company's business (if there is more than one), you may be able to determine how big the end markets are for its products.

Your company's competitors along with direct comparisons of certain metrics for both the company you're researching and its competitors. If you're still uncertain about how the company's business model works, you should look to fill in any gaps here before moving forward. Sometimes just reading about competitors may help you understand what your target company actually does.

Valuation Multiples

Now it's time to get to the nitty-gritty of performing due diligence on a stock. You'll want to review the price/earnings to growth (PEG) ratio for both the company you're researching and its competitors. Make a note of any large discrepancies in valuations between the company and its competitors. It's not uncommon to become more interested in a competitor stock during this step, which is perfectly fine. However, follow through with the original due diligence while noting the other company for further review down the road.

Management and Ownership

As part of performing due diligence on a stock, you'll want to answer some key questions regarding the company's management and ownership. Is the company still run by its founders? Or have management and the board shuffled in a lot of new faces? The age of the company is a big factor here, as younger companies tend to have more of the founding members still around. Look at consolidated bios of top managers to see what kind of broad experiences they have. You can find this information on the company's website or in its Securities and Exchange Commission (SEC) filings.

Also look to see if founders and managers hold a high proportion of shares, and what amount of the float is held by institutions. Institutional ownership percentages indicate how much analyst coverage the company is getting as well as factors influencing trade volumes. Consider high personal ownership by top managers as a plus, and low ownership a potential red flag. Shareholders tend to be best served when the people running the company have a stake in the performance of the stock.

Balance Sheet Exam

Many articles could easily be devoted to how to do a balance sheet review, but for our initial due diligence purposes, a cursory exam will do. Review your company's consolidated balance sheet to see the overall level of assets and liabilities, paying special attention to cash levels (the ability to pay short-term liabilities) and the amount of long-term debt held by the company. A lot of debt is not necessarily a bad thing and depends more on the company's business model than anything else.

Some companies (and industries as a whole) are very capital intensive, while others require little more than the basics of employees, equipment, and a novel idea to get up and running. Look at the debt-to-equity ratio to see how much positive equity the company has. You can then compare this with the competitors' debt-to-equity ratios to put the metric into a better perspective.

Stock Price History

At this point, you'll want to nail down just how long all classes of shares have been trading, as well as both short-term and long-term price movement. Has the stock price been choppy and volatile, or smooth and steady? This outlines what kind of profit experience the average owner of the stock has seen, which can influence future stock movement. Stocks that are continuously volatile tend to have short-term shareholders, which can add extra risk factors to certain investors.

Risks

Setting this vital piece aside for the end makes sure that we're always emphasizing the risks inherent with investing. Make sure to understand both industry-wide risks and company-specific ones. Are there outstanding legal or regulatory matters? Is management making decisions that lead to an increase in the company's revenues? Is the company eco-friendly? What kind of long-term risks could result from it embracing/not embracing green initiatives? Investors should keep a healthy devil's advocate mindset at all times, picturing worst-case scenarios and their potential outcomes on the stock.

Lessons from an investing legend

Former Fidelity fund manager Peter Lynch shares some of his secrets to success.

In the early 1980s, a young portfolio manager named Peter Lynch was becoming one of the most famous investors in the world, and for a very understandable reason – when he took over the Fidelity Magellan mutual fund in May of 1977 (his first job as a portfolio manager), the assets of the fund were $20 million. He proceeded to turn it into the largest mutual fund in the world, outperforming the market by a mind-boggling 13.4% per year annualized!

Know What You Own

IGOI and GEOY were prime examples of investing in what I saw and used in normal day to day life.

Your investor's edge is not something you get from Wall Street experts. It's something you already have. You can outperform the experts if you use your edge by investing in companies or industries you already understand.

Never invest in any idea you can't illustrate with a crayon.

Behind Every Stock is Company

I think you have to learn that there's a company behind every stock, and that there's only one real reason why stocks go up. Companies go from doing poorly to doing well or small companies grow to large companies.

Although it's easy to forget sometimes, a share is not a lottery ticket… it's part-ownership of a business.

Invest in Quality Companies

Go for a business that any idiot can run – because sooner or later, any idiot probably is going to run it.

Lynch's seminal book, One Up on Wall Street, articulates his investment philosophy. The Lynch stock-picking approach has several key principles: First, you should invest only in what you understand. Second, you should do your homework and research an investment thoroughly. Third, you should focus more on a company's fundamentals and not the market as a whole. Last, you should invest only for the long run and discard short-term market gyrations. If you adhere to the basic principles of this investment philosophy, Lynch believes that you will be well on your way to "beating the street."

Peter Lynch's aim was to buy good quality companies that Wall Street has ignored.

These companies have strong earnings growth with solid balance sheets and sooner or later these growing companies are noticed by Wall Street and their stock price explodes.

What's the biggest mistake you see individual investors making?

Lynch: the public's careful when they buy a house, when they buy a refrigerator, when they buy a car. They'll work hours to save a hundred dollars on a roundtrip air ticket. They'll put $5,000 or $10,000 on some zany idea they heard on the bus. That's gambling. That's not investing. That's not research. That's just total speculation.

How should individual investors approach picking stocks?

Lynch: Stocks aren't lottery tickets. Behind every stock is a company. If the company does well, over time the stocks do well, and vice versa. You have to look at the company—that's what you research. That's what we do at Fidelity, and that's what I do.

What's a good way to begin investing in stocks?

Lynch: Start with a paper portfolio. Then say: I'm going to put together X amount of dollars in the portfolio—say $10,000 or $100,000. It's paper. Make it big. Pick 5 companies to buy. Then ask why am I buying these 5? It's not "the sucker's going up." I've tried that one. That's not the reason. What is the reason why I like this?

Then you follow them over time and see what you're good at. Are you good at turn-arounds? Are you good at value stocks? Good at smaller companies?

The important thing is not the fact that the stock went from $3 to $6. Why did it go up? What happened to the story? That's what research is about. Did the company's fundamentals get better?

How can an average investor get an edge?

Lynch: Ask yourself: Can I analyze the company? Everybody has a good idea of what McDonald's does. But it's hard to analyze biotechnology companies or computer software companies. So ask yourself: Do you know something about the company? What can you add to the math? Do you have an edge?

You could be an interventional cardiologist and you put in a heart pump. You say, wow, this really is an incredible breakthrough, preventing shock, providing hemodynamic support. You're actually in the operating room, seeing this breakthrough way ahead of most people. That's an edge. You need an edge on something.

What do you look for when shopping for stocks to buy?

Lynch: In baseball terms, you want to buy in the second or third inning and get out in the seventh or eighth.

Walmart was in only 15% of the United States when they were a 10-year-old public company. All they did for the next 30 years was go from 15% to 100%. The stock went up 50-fold. They had a great formula, and they just rolled with it in the United States.

"I owned Dunkin Donuts for 12 years. I think I might have talked to them once every year. The story didn't change a lot. You don't have to worry about low-cost imports coming from Korea, when you own a donut company. You don't have to worry about the economy. You don't have to worry about someone investing a new computer chip. The story doesn't change that much." Lynch

"The stock market is a long-term investment. If you need to use the money anytime soon, you should not invest in stocks. This is the money you are willing to put in the market and leave it there for 5, 10, 20, 30 years. That is the kind of money you can do well with. If you are worried about it, don't invest it." Lynch

"You shouldn't be intimidated. Everyone can do well in the stock market. You have the skills. You have the intelligence. It doesn't require any education. All you have to have is patience, do a little research, you have got it. Don't worry about it. Don't panic.

A Good Story

You can't just go out and buy a stock and hope it goes up. You have to have a reason why you think a stock will go up. You should be able to tell those reasons to someone else in just a few minutes. People who love stocks don't talk about sports, they don't talk about their dog, and they talk about stories. A story is what is happening inside a company and signs that point to what is likely to happen in the future. I will be able to put it down in two paragraphs. It could be something like earnings are turning around, a new product, somebody's gone out of business that was competing with them, they have just discovered oil, they have a new management, is their balance sheets getting better, they are getting rid of a losing division. There is a lot of different elements, but that's what a story is and that's what you rely on.

A good story is one that you could tell a fifth grader and he or she would understand. The more complicated the story more likely it is to fall apart. You just need one good simple story to buy a stock and then follow that story. Read through the story that I wrote for Toys "R" Us back in 1978. You didn't need a degree from Business School to realize this company had a great formula and had lots of room to grow. The thousands of people who shopped there knew the store was great. I did the rest of the research I needed to fill in the story and bought the stock. Building stories like this one is how I decide what companies to own and which ones to stay away from. Remember that stories unfold over time. Companies are never stagnant. So, you have to stay tuned and sometimes make adjustments. Just like playing seven card stud poker or perhaps twenty-seven card stud poker, at the beginning of the game you only know some of the cards. You must place your bet accordingly. As each new card is revealed the game changes. You are forced to alter your betting strategy, perhaps even drop out of the game altogether.

Before you buy stock and done the Due Diligence of the company, some questions need to be answered before buying stock.

Q&A

- **What does company do?**
- **Your Answer**

- **Who are the founders?**
- **Your Answer**

- **Year of incorporation and place?**
- **Your Answer**

- **How company generate revenue?**
- **Your Answer**

- Who are the customers?
- Your Answer

- Who are the Suppliers?
- Your Answer

- Which location company operate in?
- Your Answer

- Who are the competitors?
- Your Answer

- Do company have barrier to entry?
- Your Answer

- What is the market share of the company?
- Your Answer

- Compare company growth with industry growth?
- Your Answer

- Does company buyback stock and distribute dividend?
- Your Answer

- Does company management rational?
- Your Answer

- **How company grow such as through organic or acquisition?**
- **Your Answer**

This kind of approach you need, when you select a company to invest, the main reason to invest is to gain a return, the investment return is based on your Research and Due Diligence, you must be very confident and comfortable enough that you have understood the company ecosystem and comfortable enough to invest your hard-earned money.

Invest only in a company you understand and fundamentally sound stocks have a transparent and robust business model and professionally well-managed. Such companies can survive any economic downturns and are usually the first to recover and outperform as when the economy improves.

There are an infinite number of reasons you might decide to invest in a certain company. But Berkshire Hathaway CEO Warren Buffett says there's one you should always avoid: Buying a stock merely because you think it's going to increase in price. That's because even the best investors aren't able to predict how the market will perform.

Instead, you should invest in companies that you both understand and believe will offer long-term value, according to Buffett.

No matter how much or how little you're buying, you should be able to get your reasoning down on paper without relying on outside resources, Buffett told Becky Quick on CNBC's "Squawk Box".

"Everybody when they buy a stock should be able to take a yellow pad" and write down exactly why they plan to invest in that particular company, Buffett said.

He also doesn't think investors should worry about how the stock will perform in the near term. If you want to predict what the stock price is going to do, "you can have a separate piece of paper," he said. Rather, Buffett recommends focusing on businesses that will hold their value over time. As he told CNBC in 2018, "nobody buys a farm based on whether they think it's going to rain next year."

"You're buying businesses," Buffett told quickly. Because people can "make decisions every second with stocks," as opposed to investing in a physical entity like stores or farms, "they think an investment in stocks is different than an investment in a business. But it isn't."

2

Investor or Trader

Most of the investor, don't know he is a trader or an investor, all he need a good return, most trader are investor but not all investor are traders. Investor make money for himself and trader make money for brokerage firm and to pay taxes to the government. You need to ask yourself, are you an investor or a trader?

Stock Market Investing vs Trading

Investing	Trading
Longer term, slower growth, buy and hold (years to decades)	Shorter term frequent buying and selling with the goal of outperforming buy and hold returns.
In the mindset of being "part of the company"	
Much less sensitive to short term price fluctuations	Sensitive to short term price fluctuations.
Compounding (reinvesting profits and dividends into more shares)	More paid in commissions due to many transactions
More concerned with market and company fundamentals (P/E Ratios, cash flow, etc	Technical analysis based (Chart patterns, indicators, etc)
Famous Investor Warren Buffet	Famous Trader Jesse Livermore

Investing and trading are two very different methods of attempting to profit in the financial markets. Both investors and traders seek profits through market participation. In general, investors seek larger returns over an extended period through buying and holding. Traders, by contrast, take advantage of both rising and falling markets to enter and exit positions over a shorter timeframe, taking smaller, more frequent profits.

A trader's style refers to the timeframe or holding period in which stocks, commodities, or other trading instruments are bought and sold. Traders generally fall into one of four categories:

- Position Trader: Positions are held from months to years.
- Swing Trader: Positions are held from days to weeks.
- Day Trader: Positions are held throughout the day only with no overnight positions.
- Scalp Trader: Positions are held for seconds to minutes with no overnight positions.

At times people consider themselves as long term investor when investing for 6 months to 1 year and this is reference to the sales person who helped you open your brokerage account. No business can turn things around in 6 months to one year. Any business needs time and so according to me it is at least 5 years (at times even more) and so if you are buying an undervalued company for investment, it should be given few years to turn the things around and to reflect the same in the stock price. So investment in market less than 5 years is trading.

So now the question to you as well – Are you a trader or investor?

Investor Warren Buffett

A staunch believer in the value-based investing model, investment guru Warren Buffett has long held the belief that people should only buy stocks in companies that exhibit solid fundamentals, strong earnings power, and the potential for continued growth. Although these seem like simple concepts, detecting them is not always easy. Fortunately, Buffet has developed a list of tenets that help him employ his investment philosophy to maximum effect.

- Warren Buffett is noted for introducing the value investing philosophy to the masses, advocating investing in companies that show robust earnings and long-term growth potential.
- To granularly drill down on his analysis, Buffett has identified several core tenets, in the categories of business, management, financial measures, and value.
- Buffett favors companies that distribute dividend earnings to shareholders and is drawn to transparent companies that cop to their mistakes.

"The Warren Buffett Portfolio" is a timeless book that offers valuable insight into the psychological mindset of the legendary investor, Warren Buffett. Of course, if learning how to invest like Warren Buffett was as easy as reading a book, everyone would be rich! But if you take that time and effort to implement some of Buffett's proven strategies, you could be on your way to better stock selection and greater returns.

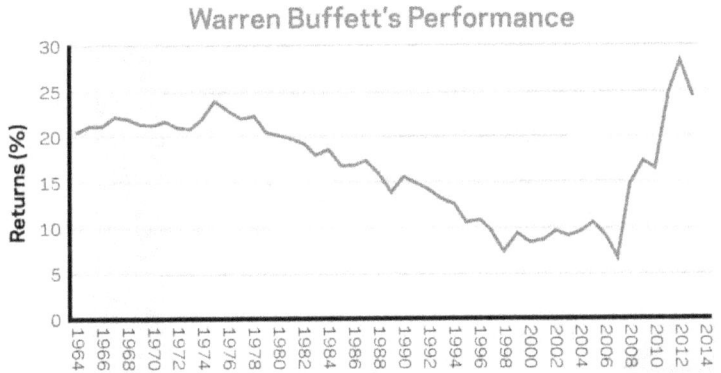

In this plot you can see the return of Warren Buffett.

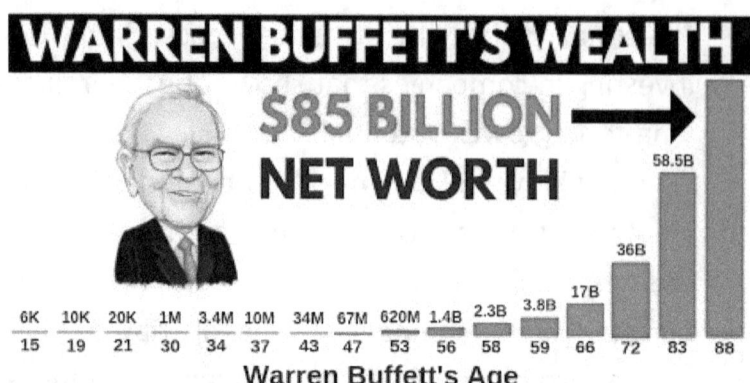

Trader Jesse Livermore

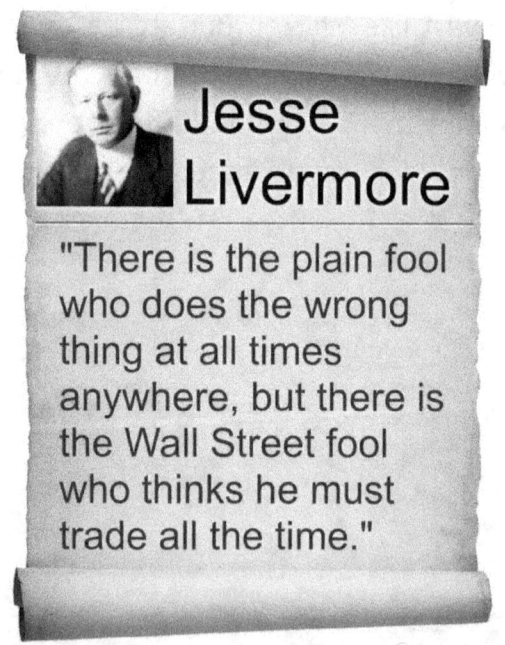

Jesse Livermore was born in 1877 and he is probably considered one of the most famous trader in history. He started trading at the age of 14 from bucket shops (an unauthorized office for speculating in stocks or currency using the funds of unwitting investors). His tape reading skill was so good that these bucket shops eventually didn't want to do business with him.

Jesse Livermore led a life of brilliance and excess, surrounded by mistresses, scandals, money, and bankruptcy. He was a legendary trader who played big and made millions during the crash of 1929.

At his peak in 1929, he was worth $100 million. Ultimately, he lost his entire fortune when he broke his trading rules. As a matter of fact the same trading rules which made him millions caused him to lose everything, when he lost control of himself.

By 1934, Livermore would have depleted the $100 million fortune he earned on the stock market just five years earlier. He declared a third bankruptcy, went through his second divorce, and committed suicide in 1940 — the newspapers then detailing his scandals rather than the achievements of his earlier days.

On November 27, 1940, Jesse Livermore and his wife, Harriet, went to New York's Stork Club, where a photographer asked permission to take a picture. "It's the last picture you'll take of me. Tomorrow I'm going away for a long, long time," Livermore said.

This is what Jesse Livermore wrote in his suicide note to his wife:

My dear Nina: Canât help it. Things have been bad with me. I am tired of fighting. Canât carry on any longer. This is the only way out. I am unworthy of your love. I am a failure. I am truly sorry, but this is the only way out for me. Love Laurie"

"Black Tuesday"

- Stock market crashes on Oct. 29, 1929
- Brokers could not sell stocks, many worthless

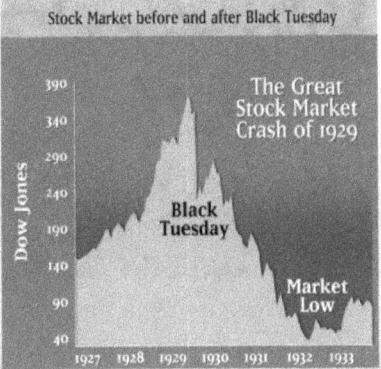

A man must know himself thoroughly if he is going to make a good job out of trading in the speculative markets. To know what I was capable of in the line of folly was a long educational step. I sometimes think that no price is too high for a speculator to pay to learn that which will keep him from getting the swelled head."
— Jesse Livermore, Reminiscences of a Stock Operator

Return of Investor vs. Trader

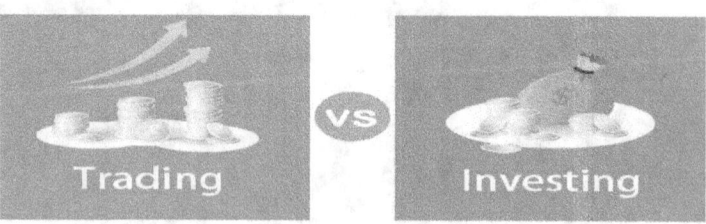

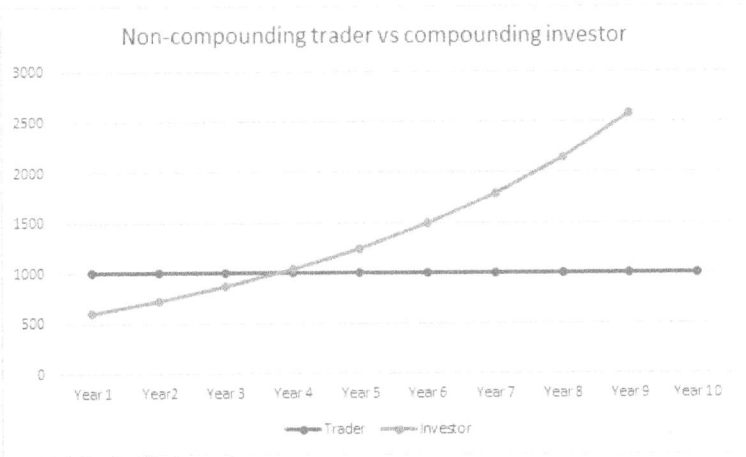

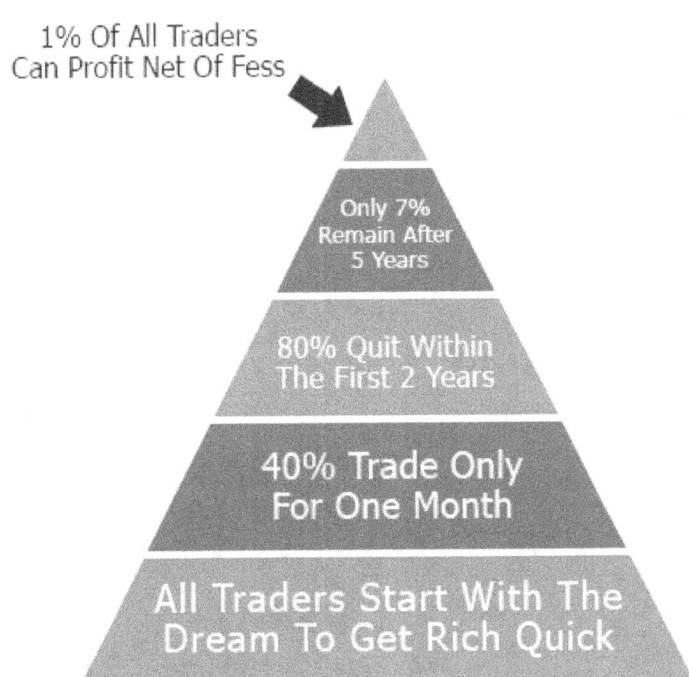

Lesson from Mountaineer Edmund Viesturs

Edmund Viesturs is a high-altitude mountaineer and corporate speaker. He is the only American to have climbed all 14 of the world's eight-thousander mountain peaks, and the fifth person to do so without using supplemental oxygen. Along with Apa Sherpa, he has summitted peaks of over 8,000 meters on 21 occasions, including Mount Everest seven times; only four other climbers, Phurba Tashi Sherpa Mendewa, Juanito Oiarzabal, Namgyal Sherpa, and Ang Dorje Sherpa, have more high-altitude ascents.

Viesturs took part in the 1996 IMAX filming of Everest shortly after the 1996 Mount Everest disaster, which became the highest grossing documentary up to that time. Thirteen days after the disaster, his team summited Everest accompanied by a film crew. He also had a cameo in the year 2000 Hollywood blockbuster Vertical Limit. Clive Standen plays Viesturs in the 2015 remake of Everest telling of the 1996 Mount Everest disaster.

His Book

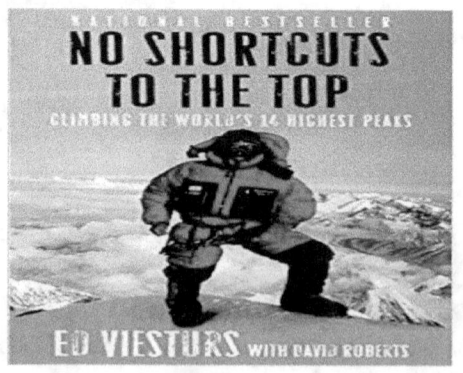

For eighteen years Ed Viesturs pursued climbing's holy grail: to stand atop the world's fourteen 8,000-meter peaks, without the aid of bottled oxygen. But No Shortcuts to the Top is as much about the man who would become the first American to achieve that goal as it is about his stunning quest. As Viesturs recounts the stories of his most harrowing climbs, he reveals a man torn between the flat, safe world he and his loved ones share and the majestic and deadly places where only he can go.

A preternaturally cautious climber who once turned back 300 feet from the top of Everest but who would not shrink from a peak (Annapurna) known to claim the life of one climber for every two who reached its summit, Viesturs lives by an unyielding motto, "Reaching the summit is optional. Getting down is mandatory." It is with this philosophy that he vividly describes fatal errors in judgment made by his fellow climbers as well as a few of his own close calls and gallant rescues. And, for the first time, he details his own pivotal and heroic role in the 1996 Everest disaster made famous in Jon Krakauer's Into Thin Air.

Getting Down is Mandatory

Along the pathway to success, Viesturs has tasted bitter setbacks. During a climb of Mount Everest, he and his team were 300 feet from the summit. And then he noticed a change in the weather. Conditions were ripe for a potential avalanche. He realized that if the team pressed on to the top of the mountain, they wouldn't have time to make it down. His trademark phrase came from this experience: "Getting to the summit is optional, getting down is mandatory. It has to be a round trip." Viesturs and team turned around and they went back home. And they lived to scale Everest another day.

In investment world, you need to be a long term investor to be wealthy .If you trade; you are making your investment and your life in risk.

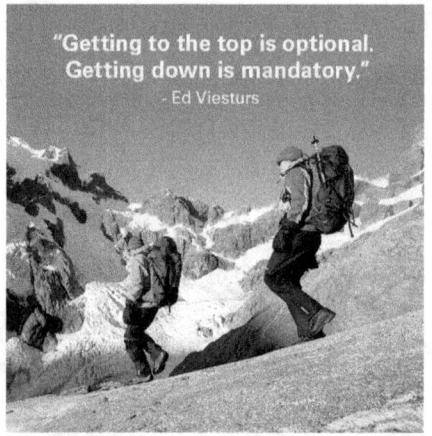

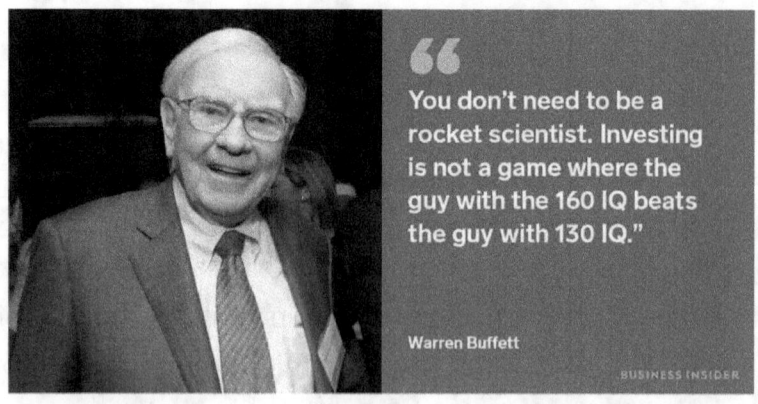

- *What do you see?*
- *Books*
- *Reading*
- *Net worth $ 88 Billion*
- *No Computer*

Tod Combs & Teds , Warren buffett Money Manager

What today B-School have access to a state of the art Bloomberg Terminal within the campus.

This is how they teach investing, are they going to be a Billionaire? Their Net Worth?

Technical chat of a company will never tell you the story behind the company fundamentals; you have to dive into to financial of the company to know the truth.

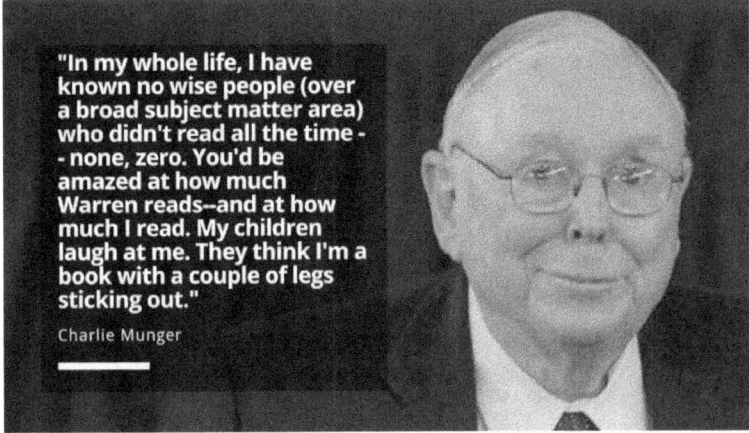

Q&A

- Are you an Investor or Trader?
- Your Answer

- Investor makes money for whom?
- Your Answer - Himself or Broker

- Jesse Livermore is a?
- Your Answer - Investor or Trader

- Which year is a Black Tuesday in Wall Street?
- Your Answer -

- Which have high return Investor vs. Trader?
- Your Answer -

- What is Trader Survival Rate?
- Your Answer -

- Who said Getting to the summit is optional, getting down is mandatory?
- Your Answer -

- Can you read like Warren Buffett or using terminal to forecast the future of stock?
- Your Answer -

3

Competitive Industry

Time is the friend of the wonderful company, the enemy of the mediocre.
~ Warren Buffett

Most of the investor never figures it out about the industry competitions and they invest in the poor and highly competitive industry those results in poor return or a negative return.

One of essential components of a competitive industry is the presence of many different sellers of a particular good or service and many potential buyers. If a particular seller controls a large proportion of the market for a certain good or service, it may have the power to set the price for the product or service higher than it would if there were more competitors. In a perfectly competitive industry sellers do not they determine the price of goods or services: the price is determined by market. When demand for a certain product or service is high in a competitive market, price will tend to rise, and when demand is low, prices will tend to fall.

Lesson from Warren Buffett

DOW JONES INDUSTRIAL AVERAGE December 31, 1964 874.12 December 31, 1981 875.00 He walked over to the screen and started explaining. "During these seventeen years, the size of the economy grew fivefold. The sales of the Fortune five hundred companies grew more than fivefold.*2 Yet, during these seventeen years, the stock market went exactly nowhere." He backed up a step or two. "What you're doing when you invest is deferring consumption and laying money out now to get more money back at a later time. And there are really only two questions. One is how much you're going to get back, and the other is when. "Now, Aesop was not much of finance major, because he said something like, 'A bird in the hand is worth two in the bush.' But he doesn't say when." Interest rates—the cost of borrowing—Buffett explained, are the price of "when." They are to finance as gravity is to physics. As interest rates vary, the value of all financial assets—houses, stocks, bonds—changes, as if the price of birds had fluctuated. "And that's why sometimes a bird in the hand is better than two birds in the bush and sometimes two in the bush are better than one in the hand."

"This is half of a page which comes from a list seventy pages long of all the auto companies in the United States." He waved the complete list in the air. "There were two thousand auto companies: the most important invention, probably, of the first half of the twentieth century. It had an enormous impact on people's lives. If you had seen at the time of the first cars how this country would develop in connection with autos, you would have said, 'This is the place I must be.' But of the two thousand companies, as of a few years ago, only three car companies survived. And, at one time or another, all three were selling for less than book value, which is the amount of money that had been put into the companies and left there. So autos had an enormous impact on America, but in the opposite direction on investors." He put down the list to shove his hand in his pocket. "Now, sometimes it's much easier to figure out the losers. There was, I think, one obvious decision back then. And of course, the thing you should have been doing was shorting horses.

U.S. HORSE POPULATION 1900—17 million 1998—5 million "Frankly, I'm kind of disappointed that the Buffett family was not shorting horses throughout this entire period. There are always losers."

"Now the other great invention of the first half of the century was the airplane. In this period from 1919 to 1939, there were about two hundred companies. Imagine if you could have seen the future of the airline industry back there at Kitty Hawk. You would have seen a world undreamed of. But assume you had the insight, and you saw all of these people wishing to fly and to visit their relatives or run away from their relatives or whatever you do in an airplane, and you decided this was the place to be. "As of a couple of years ago, there had been zero money made from the aggregate of all stock investments in the airline industry in history."

Now he was talking about their businesses. "It's wonderful to promote new industries, because they are very promotable. It's very hard to promote investment in a mundane product. It's much easier to promote an esoteric product, even particularly one with losses, because there's no quantitative guideline." This was goring the audience directly, where it hurt. "But people will keep coming back to invest, you know. It reminds me a little of that story of the oil prospector who died and went to heaven. And St. Peter said, 'Well, I checked you out, and you meet all of the qualifications. But there's one problem.' He said, 'We have some tough zoning laws up here, and we keep all of the oil prospectors over in that pen. And as you can see, it is absolutely chock-full. There is no room for you.' "And the prospector said, 'Do you mind if I just say four words?' "St. Peter said, 'No harm in that.' "So the prospector cupped his hands and yells out, 'Oil discovered in hell!' "And of course, the lock comes off the cage and all of the oil prospectors start heading right straight down. "St. Peter said, 'That's a pretty slick trick. So,' he says, 'go on in, make yourself at home. All the room in the world.' "The prospector paused for a minute, then said, 'No, I think I'll go along with the rest of the boys. There might be some truth to that rumor after all.' 23 "Well, that's the way people feel with stocks. It's very easy to believe that there's some truth to that rumor after all."

Lesson from Peter Lynch

Peter Lynch: I will speak about some of the ideas I used when I was an amateur, when I ran Magellan, and which I still use today. They can make sense for investors.

It's a tragedy in America that small investors have been convinced by the media – the print media, radio, television media – they don't have a chance. These media giants have convinced many small investors they can't compete with big institutions – with all their computers and degrees and money. It just isn't true.

His single most important thing to me in the stock market for anyone is to know what you own. I'm amazed how many people who own stocks would not be able to tell you why they own them. If you press them, they'll say, "The reason I own this is because the sucker's going up." That's the only reason they own it. I'm serious. If you can't explain to a 10-year-old in two minutes or less why you own a stock, you shouldn't own it. That's true of about 80% of people who own stocks.

This is the stock people like to own. This is the company people adore owning. These are relatively simple companies, and they make a narrow, easy-to-understand product. They make a one-megabit, SRAM, CMOS, bi-polar risk, floating point data IO array processor, with an optimized compiler, a 16-bit dual-port memory, a double-defused metal oxide semiconductor monolithic logic chip with a plasma matrix vacuum fluorescent display with a 16-bit dual memory with a UNIX operating system, four whetstone megaflop poly-silicone emitter, a high bandwidth – that's important – six-gigahertz double metallization communication protocol, an asynchronous backward compatibility, peripheral bus architecture, four-way interleaf memory, a token ring interchanging backplane, and it does it in 15 nanoseconds of capability. If you own a piece of crap like that, you will never make money. Somebody will come along with more whetstones or less whetstones, a bigger megaflop or a smaller megaflop. You won't have the foggiest idea what's happening, and people buy this junk all the time.

I made money in Dunkin' Donuts. I can understand it. When there were recessions, I didn't have to worry about what was happening. I could go there, and people were still there, I didn't have to worry about low-priced Korean imports. I can understand it. And you laugh. I made 10 or 15 times my money in Dunkin' Donuts. Those are the stocks I can understand. If you don't understand it, it doesn't work. This is the single biggest principle.

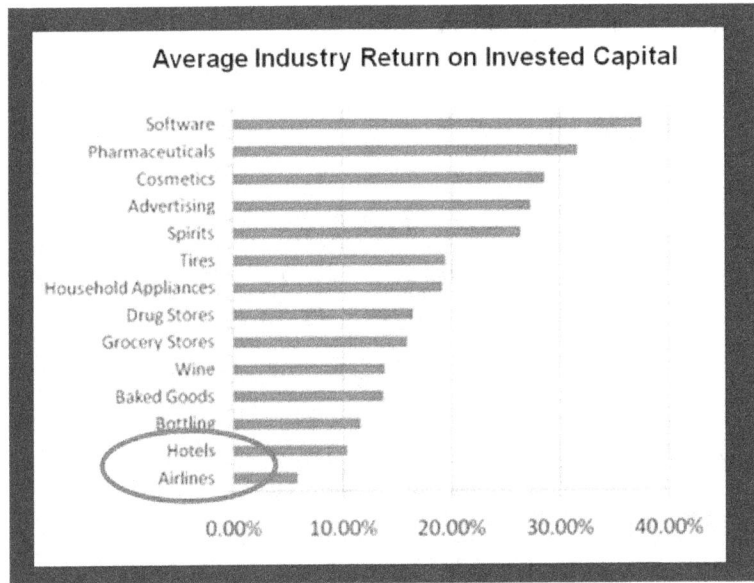

In a competitive industry, firms must offer products that are similar enough to one another to be considered interchangeable. For instance, a company that sells baseballs might not be in direct competition with a company that sells softballs, even though the balls are somewhat similar, because a baseball is not a substitute for a softball.

What is the market? Market is a place and sellers come face to face with buyers in that place. But communication and transportation revolution changes it from a place Todays technology makes it an "environmental." Seller or buyers can supply or demand any goods with phone, fax or internet. The market lost its concrete pattern. Economists divide to the market into two parts. These are; perfectly competitive market and imperfectly competitive market. I

One of the types of imperfect competition is monopoly markets. It is a kind of market which is far from perfect competition market. There is only one producer/seller for a product so the single business is the industry. Difficult to enter such a market and requires high cost. There are economic, social and political boundaries of these markets. For example, if a government wants to control, such as electricity, it can be create a monopoly over that industry.

Monopoly market gives to its owners some special rights and privileges for an asset or a natural resource. For example, in Saudi Arabia, the government has sole control over the oil industry. There is no fear of seller from any competing firms. Because of there is not another company that produces same goods or supply of same goods. Therefore monopoly firms move in independence about sale price, for a value investor love to invest in this industry such as Microsoft, Apple, face book, they enjoy the market share.

The type is perfect competition market, the buyers and sellers cannot influence to price alone in that market. In other words firms cannot apply to independent price policy under the perfect competition. Price is evident and companies have to accept it. This is shown with horizontal price line. There are a lot of sellers in that market who produce the same goods and there are a lot of buyers in that market who want to buy the same goods.

If a firm increases or decreases to its amount of sales, the price of goods won't change too much. Because of there are many vendors in that market .In the other words, each company must accept as the market price. Investor should avoid such kind of industry such as Airlines, Automobiles. In this industry many businesses declare bankruptcy every day.

1. Large number of buyers and sellers.

2. Homogenous product is produced by every firm.

3. Free entry and exit of firms.

4. Zero advertising cost.

5. Consumers have perfect knowledge about the market and are well aware of any changes in the market. Consumers indulge in rational decision making.

6. All the factors of production, viz. labour, capital, etc, have perfect mobility in the market and are not hindered by any market factors or market forces.

7. No government intervention.

8. No transportation costs.

9. Each firm earns normal profits and no firms can earn super-normal profits.

10. Every firm is a price taker. It takes the price as decided by the forces of demand and supply. No firm can influence the price of the product.

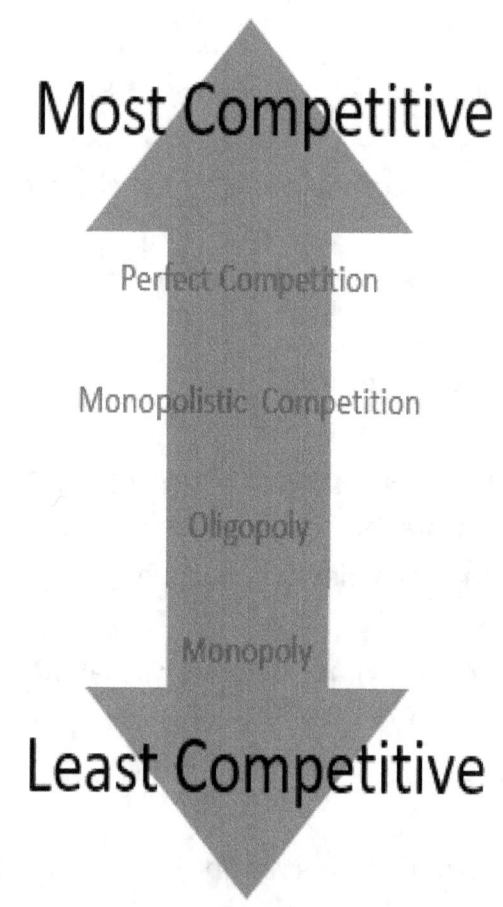

Look for a company in Least Competitive Industry

Equal price prevails in the whole perfect competitive market.
Buyer or Seller cannot influence the price.
In Perfect Competition, a firm is a **'Price Taker'** and Industry is a **'Price Maker'**.

Revenue of Perfect Competitive Firm

Price (P) ₹	Quantity (Q) ₹	Total Revenue (TR) ₹	Average Revenue (AR) ₹	Marginal Revenue (MR) ₹
5	1	5	5	5
5	2	10	5	5
5	3	15	5	5
5	4	20	5	5
5	5	25	5	5

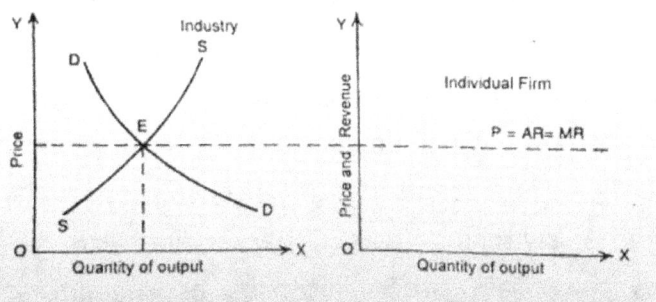

- Industry where demand intersect the supply, that is E, the set price by the industry not by the company.
- Individual firm P=AR=MR is same, company need to follow the price of the product set by the industry.

The perfect competition doesn't exist in our world today, it would be nearly impossible. But theoretically, it would be a perfect competition between businesses. If we had a perfect competition, a good example would be the automobile industry. Instead of seeing a different car on every turn, we would just see one. All car companies like Ford, Honda, and Chevy, would all sell the exact same cars. All cars would be the same, all the prices would be the same for each car, and there would be no competition. It wouldn't matter if you went to the Ford dealership or the Honda dealership. You could get the exact same car, for the exact same price.

What Are Barriers to Entry?

Barriers to entry are the economic term describing the existence of high start-up costs or other obstacles that prevent new competitors from easily entering an industry or area of business. Barriers to entry benefit existing firms because they protect their revenues and profits. Common barriers to entry include special tax benefits to existing firms, patents, strong brand identity or customer loyalty, and high customer switching costs. Others include the need for new firms to obtain proper licenses or regulatory clearance before operation.

Type of market structure	Level of barriers to entry
Perfect competition	Zero barriers to entry
Monopolistic competition	Medium barriers to entry
Oligopoly	High barriers to entry
Monopoly	Very high to absolute barriers to entry

Economies of scale: If a market has significant economies of scale that have already been exploited by the existing firms to a large extent, new entrants are deterred. When more units of a good or service can be produced on a larger scale, yet with (on average) fewer input costs, economies of scale are said to be achieved.

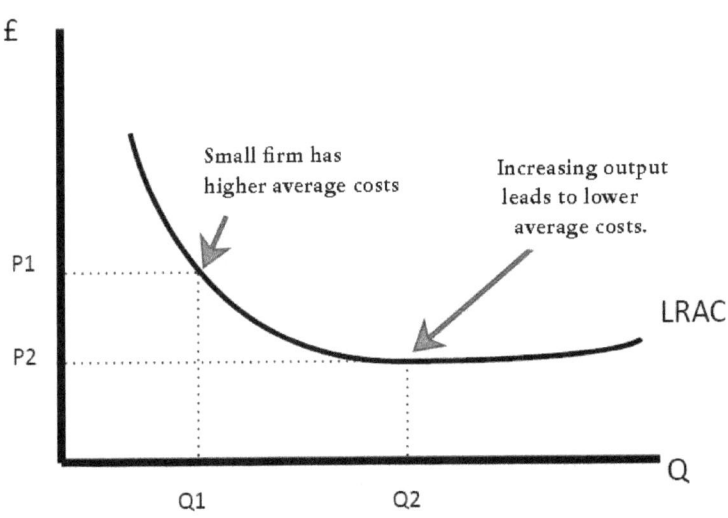

As an investor you should invest in a company which has barrier to entry and enjoy monopoly, competitive advantage. Most of the investor don't know much about the company , how they manufacture and what will be cost per unit , if you see above the plot , it state that when a firm increase the quantity , the cost of production per unit decrease and firm can in increase the gross profit margins with demand increase.

News May 2020 Airline Stocks Amid Coronavirus: 'I Made A Mistake' Warren Buffett

He had sold all of the company's airline stocks, admitting that he had made a mistake and that coronavirus had changed the business in a "very major way."

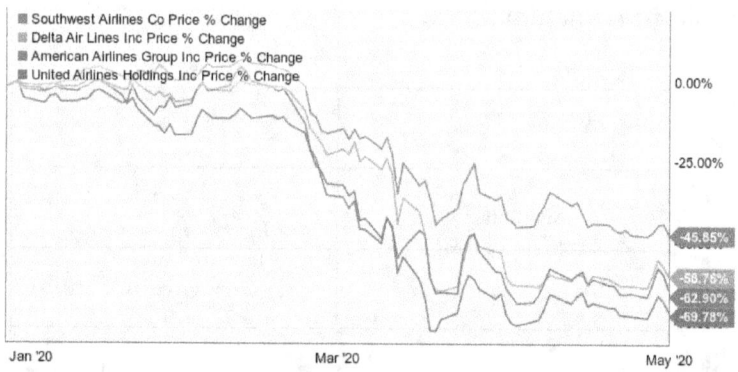

"The world has changed for airlines," Buffett said, noting that the industry has been "really hurt by a forced shutdown" due to the coronavirus.

Berkshire Hathaway reported a massive net loss of nearly $50 billion in the first quarter. The coronavirus market selloff that occurred in late February and through most of March took a significant toll on the company's businesses.

Q&A

- Can you Explain industry competitions?
- Your Answer -

- U.S. HORSE POPULATION 1900—17 million 1998?
- Your Answer -

- Other great invention of the first half of the Century was?
- Your Answer -

- How much money made from the aggregate of all stock investments in the airline industry in history?
- Your Answer -

- Value Inventor invests in which industry?
- Your Answer - Prefect Competition or imperfect competition?

4

Macro Analysis

Many of Investor try to predict the market, what will be interest rate, what will be GDP etc and they fail to understand the MICRO analysis of the company, if you are look at the MACRO factor in your investment and ignore the MICRO factor, you may end up with not making any money .Warren Buffett is famous for telling investors that he and Charlie don't pay any attention to macroeconomics and that they would be well served by ignoring macroeconomics as well.

If thing are bad now, they will get better in time. If they are fine now, something will go wrong in due course. We don't make money by predicting the timing.

At Berkshire, we're trying to swim well against the tide or with it, we just keep swimming."

We are doing things that we haven't seen in the past. And policymakers do not know the outcome of that. I don't know the outcome of it. You do know it will have consequences." --Warren Buffett (2009)

"I do not know the answer as to what happens if you keep rates close to zero for a very, very long time." --Warren Buffett (2014)

"Nobody, for instance, in Japan would ever have anticipated that interest rates would go way down and stay down for 20 years. And nobody would've expected common stocks to decline by huge amounts and stay down for 20 years. So strange things have happened. And they're very confusing to the economics profession. In fact, if you're not confused, you really probably don't understand it very well." --Charlie Munger (2014)

"We've taken the Federal Reserve balance sheet up from a trillion to over 4 trillion, and we've done a lot of things that weren't in my Economics 101 course, and so far nothing bad has happened, except for the fact that people who saved and kept their money in short-term savings instruments have just totally gotten killed, in terms of the income that they received from that. But it's still hard for me to see how if you toss money from helicopters that eventually you don't have inflation. Certainly, if the money supplied grows faster and faster relative to the output of goods and services, something like that is supposed to happen. But I've been surprised by what's happened. When Poland issues bonds at negative interest rates, you know, I did not have that in my list of forecasts a few years ago. And so I think we're operating in a world that Charlie and I don't understand very well." --Warren Buffett (2015)

"We have made very little progress in life by trying to outguess these macroeconomic factors. We basically have abdicated. We're just swimming all the time, and we let the tide take care of itself.... The trouble with making all these economic pronouncements is that people gradually get so they think they know something. It's much better just to say, 'I'm ignorant.'" --Charlie Munger (2015)

"We're interested in economic matters, and political matters, for that matter. We know a lot, or are familiar...with almost all the macroeconomic factors. That doesn't mean we know where they're going to lead. We don't know where zero interest rates are going to lead." --Warren Buffett (2016)

"I don't think anybody really knows much about negative interest rates. We never had them before. And we've never had periods of stasis like — except for the Great Depression — we didn't have things like happened in Japan: great modern nation playing all the monetary tricks, Keynesian tricks, stimulus tricks, and mired in stasis for 25 years. And none of the great economists who have studied this stuff, and taught it to our children, understand it, either. So we just do the best we can. Our advantage is that we know we don't understand it. If you're not confused, you haven't thought about it correctly. " --Charlie Munger (2016)

Think about where the business is going to be in the future – not macro factors. I have never taken a single course in economics, nor tried to make a single dollar, ever, from foreseeing macroeconomic changes. There's too much emphasis of macroeconomics and not enough on microeconomics. I think this is wrong. It's like trying to master medicine without knowing anatomy and chemistry. If you're agnostic about macro factors and, therefore, devote all of your time to thinking about individual businesses and the individual opportunities, it's a way more efficient way to behave. Macroeconomics people are often wrong because of extreme complexity in the system they wish to understand. The trouble with making all these macroeconomic predictions is that people start to think they know something. It's much better to just say you're ignorant. People have always had this craving to have someone tell them the future. Long ago, kings would hire people to read sheep guts. There's always been a market for people who pretend to know the future. Listening to today's forecasters is just as crazy as when the king hired the guy to look at the sheep guts. It happens over and over and over. It's kind of a snare and a delusion to outguess macroeconomic cycles. When the game is that tough, why not adopt the other system of swimming as competently as you can and figuring that over a long life you'll have your share of good tides and bad tides.

--Charlie Munger

Lesson from Peter Lynch

It bothers me that people are careful with their money. The public, when they buy a refrigerator, they go to Consumer Reports. They buy a microwave oven, they do that. They ask people what's the best radar range or what car to buy. They do research on apartments. When they go on a trip to Wyoming, they get a Mobil travel guide. When they go to Europe, they get the Michelin travel guide. People hear a tip on a bus on some stock and they'll put half their life savings in it before sunset, and they wonder why they lose money in the stock market. When they lose money, they blame it on the institutions and program trading. That is garbage. They didn't do any research. They bought a piece of junk, they didn't look at the balance sheet, and that's what you get for it. That's what we're being driven to, and it's self-fulfilling. The public invests terribly, and they say they don't have a chance. It's because that's the way they're acting. I'm trying to convince people there is a method. There are reasons for stocks to go up. This is magic. It's a magic number, easy to remember. Coca-Cola is earning 30 times per share what they earned 32 years ago. The stock has gone up thirtyfold. Bethlehem Steel is earning less than they did 30 years ago. The stock is half its price of 30 years ago. Stocks are not lottery tickets. There's a company behind every stock. If a company does well, the stock does well. It's not that complicated.

People get too carried away. They try to predict the stock market. That is a total waste of time. No one can predict the stock market. They try to predict interest rates. If anybody can predict interest rates right three times in a row, they'd be a billionaire. Certainly, there's not that many billionaires on the planet. I took logic, syllogism, when I studied at Boston College. There can't be that many people who can predict interest rates because there'd be lots of billionaires, and no one can predict the economy. I know a lot of people in this room were around in 1981 and 1982 when we had a 20% prime rate with double-digit inflation, double-digit unemployment. I don't remember anybody telling me in 1981 about it. I read. I study all this stuff. I don't remember anybody telling me we'll have the worst recession since the Depression. It would be useful to know what the stock market will do. It would be terrific to know the Dow Jones average a year from now, to know we'll have a full-scale recession, or to know interest rates will be 12%. That's useful stuff. You never know it, though. You just don't get to learn it.

I've always said if you spend 14 minutes a year on economics, you've wasted 12 minutes. Now, I must be fair. I'm talking about economics in the broad scale, predicting the downturn for next year, or the upturn, or M1 and M2, 3B. All of these economic terms are less useful to me than when you talk about scrap prices. When I own auto stocks, I want to know what's happening to used car prices. When used car prices rise, it's a good indicator. When I own hotel stocks, I want to know hotel occupancies. When I own chemical stocks, I want to know what's happening to the price of ethylene. These are facts. If aluminum inventories go down five straight months, that's relevant. I can deal with that. I want to know about home affordability when I own Fannie Mae, or I own a housing stock. These are facts. There are economic facts and there are economic predictions, and economic predictions are a total waste. Alan Greenspan is an honest guy. He would tell you he can't predict interest rates. He can tell you what short rates will do in the next six months. Try and stick him on what the long-term rate will be three years from now. He'll say, "I don't have any idea." So how are you, the investor, supposed to predict interest rates if the head of the Federal Reserve can't do it?

You should study history. History teaches you the market goes down. It goes down a lot. The math is simple. There have been 93 years this century. The market has had 50 declines of 10% or more. With 50 declines in 93 years, the market falls at least 10% about once every two years. We call that a "correction," a euphemism for losing a lot of money rapidly. Of those 50 declines, 15 have been 25% or more. That's known as a "bear market." We've had 15 declines of at least 25% in 93 years, so every six years, the market has a 25% decline. That's all you need to know. You need to know the market will go down sometimes. If you're not ready for that, you shouldn't own stocks.

It's good when the market goes down. If you like a stock at $14 and it goes to $6, that's great. You understand the company. You look at the balance sheet. They're doing fine. You hope for $22; $14 to $22 is terrific, $6 to $22 is exceptional, so you take advantage of these declines. Declines happen, and no one knows when they'll happen. People tell you they predicted it, but they predicted it 53 times. You can take advantage of the volatility of the market if you understand what you own. That's a key element.

Another key element is that you have plenty of time. People are in an unbelievable rush to buy a stock. I'll give you an example of a well-known company. Walmart went public in

October of 1970. It already had a great record with 15 years' performance and a great balance sheet. You're a conservative investor. You're not sure if Walmart can make it. You want to check. You see them operate in small towns. You're afraid. They make it in seven or eight states. You want to wait until they go to more states. You keep waiting. You could have bought Walmart 10 years after it went public and made 35 times your money. If you bought it when they went public, you would have made 500 times your money, but you could have waited 10 years after it went public and made over 30 times your money. You could have waited three years after Microsoft went public and made 10 times your money. I know nothing about software. If you knew something about software, you would have said, "These guys have it. I don't care who's going to win, Compaq, IBM. I don't know who's going to win, Japanese computers. I know Microsoft, MS-DOS is the right thing.

Stocks are not a lottery ticket. There's a company behind every stock, and you can watch it. You have plenty of time. People are in an amazing rush to purchase a security. They're out of breath when they call up. You don't need to do this.

Many investors fail to analyse the Micro level and they keep focus on Macro and predicting economic, and that doesn't work in investing,

"To give up what you're doing well because of guesses about what's going to happen in some macro way just doesn't make any sense to us." ~ Warren Buffett

"If you're agnostic about those macro factors and therefore devote all your time to thinking about the individual businesses and the individual opportunities, it's a way more efficient way to behave, at least with our particular talents and lacks thereof." ~ Charlie Munger

Macroeconomics: Definition:

The term macro is derived from the Greek word 'uakpo' which means large. Macroeconomics, the other half of economics, is the study of the behavior of the economy as a whole. In other words:

"Macroeconomics deals with total or big aggregates such as national income, output and employment, total consumption, aggregate saving and aggregate investment and the general level of prices". In the words of Boulding:

"Macroeconomics deals not with individual quantities as such but with aggregates of these quantities, not with individual i.e., but with the national Income, not with individual prices but with the price level, not with Individual outputs but with the national output. It studies determination of national output and its growth overtime. It also studies the problems of recession, unemployment inflation, the balance of international payments and the policies adopted by the governments to deal with these problems".

A macro environment is the condition that exists in the economy as a whole, rather than in a particular sector or region. In general, the macro environment includes trends in the gross domestic product (GDP), inflation, employment, spending, and monetary and fiscal policy. The macro-environment is closely linked to the general business cycle as opposed to the performance of an individual business sector.

The 6 Variables of PESTLE Analysis

- **POLITICS**
  - Government type and policy
  - Funding, grants and initiatives

- **ECONOMY**
  - Inflation and interest rates
  - Labour and energy costs

- **SOCIAL**
  - Population, education, media
  - Lifestyle, fashion, culture

- **TECHNOLOGY**
  - Emerging technologies, Web
  - Information & communication

- **LEGAL**
  - Regulations and standards
  - Employment law

- **ENVIRONMENT**
  - Weather, green & ethical issues
  - Pollution, waste, recycling

1994 Berkshire Hathaway annual meeting. "A public opinion poll will just — it will not get you rich on Wall Street," Warren Buffett also said.

The investors should not make big predictions on the direction of the economy and even the stock markets, he added. Even the forecast by others on macroeconomic matters should not impact the individual stock moves, he also said at the same meeting. Buffett and his long-time business partner Charlie Munger said they especially try to not make big predictions on the direction of the overall economy and stock market nor let the forecasts from others on those macroeconomic matters influence their individual stock decisions.

Investors Need Micro, Not Macro

Microeconomics covers specific regulatory changes and competitive pressures.

By contrast, it is not even clear if investors need macroeconomics to make good decisions. Warren Buffett once called macroeconomic literature "the funny papers" and quipped "I can't think of a time when they influenced a decision about a stock or a company." Not every investor or fund manager would agree with this sentiment, but it is telling when such a prominent figure confidently disregards the entire science.

An economy is an extremely complex and dynamic system. To borrow terms from electrical engineering, it is difficult to identify real signals in macroeconomics because the data is noisy. Macroeconomists frequently disagree about how to measure effectiveness or how to make predictions. Some new economist is always popping up with a different interpretation or spin. This makes it easy for investors to draw incorrect conclusions or even adopt contradictory indicators.

Investor should understand the Micro economics of the business.

Quantitative and Qualitative Fundamental Analysis

The problem with defining the word fundamentals is that it can cover anything related to the economic well-being of a company. They obviously include numbers like revenue and profit, but they can also include anything from a company's market share to the quality of its management.

The various fundamental factors can be grouped into two categories: quantitative and qualitative. The financial meaning of these terms isn't much different from their standard definitions. Here is how a dictionary defines the terms:

Quantitative – capable of being measured or expressed in numerical terms.

Qualitative – related to or based on the quality or character of something, often as opposed to its size or quantity.

In this context, quantitative fundamentals are hard numbers. They are the measurable characteristics of a business. That's why the biggest source of quantitative data is financial statements. Revenue, profit, assets, and more can be measured with great precision.

One of the primary assumptions of fundamental analysis is that the currently price from the stock market often does not fully reflect a value of the company supported by the publicly available data. A second assumption is that the value reflected from the company's fundamental data is more likely to be closer to a true value of the stock.

Analysts often refer to this hypothetical true value as the intrinsic value. However, it should be noted that this usage of the phrase intrinsic value means something different in stock valuation than what it means in other contexts such as options trading. Option pricing uses a standard calculation for intrinsic value; however analysts use a various complex models to arrive at their intrinsic value for a stock. There is not a single, generally accepted formula for arriving at the intrinsic value of a stock.

Q&A

- **Can you predict GDP or Interest Rate? Not waste time in this.**
- Your Answer -

- **Can you explain Micro approach about company you like to invest?**
- Your Answer -

- Do you know any Billionaire invest in learning about Macro Analysis and not Micro Analysis?
- Your Answer -

5

Mediocre Business

Ninety-five percent of startups fail within five years. The pain of business failure can be awful; but there is another pain that affects many businesses: the pain of business mediocrity. The dull, lingering torture of mediocrity can be just as soul-crushing, only the pain lasts much longer.

Berkshire Hathaway's investment in American Airlines stock was always somewhat strange given the airline's high debt and below-average margins. Yet the other three airlines had solid track records for free cash flow production prior to Berkshire getting involved. Given the structural changes to the U.S. airline industry (mainly consolidation), Buffett wasn't totally irrational to think that airlines had matured into high-quality businesses.

But as Buffett wrote in Berkshire Hathaway's 2001 annual letter, "... You only find out who is swimming naked when the tide goes out." The tide has gone out in a big way for airlines in 2020. Demand has virtually evaporated. The result was that even industry stalwarts like Southwest and Delta -- which have earned consistently high margins in recent years -- lost money last quarter and are bracing for even bigger losses ahead. American and (to a lesser extent) United have had more mixed track records over the past few years and are even worse off now.

Buffett's recent venture into and out of airline stocks can best be explained in two sentences from Berkshire Hathaway's 1987 shareholder letter: "Our goal is to find an outstanding business at a sensible price, not a mediocre business at a bargain price. ... Of course, Charlie and I may misread the fundamental economics of a business." Airlines appeared to be high-quality businesses for most of the past few years. Today, they seem far more speculative in nature, making it natural for Buffett to admit his mistake and sell Berkshire's airline stocks.

Investor should look for a company which has durable competitive advantage .A durable competitive advantage are the factors that differentiate the products and services of a company from its peers. A durable competitive advantage can be achieved by creating a strong brand, strong supply chain, wide distribution network and competitive pricing. A durable competitive advantage allows a company to capture bigger market share in its sector, maintain customer loyalty, and give pricing power on the product which helps company gain higher profit margin on products.

For Example, Nestle India Maggi brand makes multiple products such as instant noodles, and sauce. The sauce of Maggi have captured almost 50% market share because of its product quality, targeting right consumer segment (which is urban and semi urban middle class), strong distribution network which makes products available even in smaller cities, and continuous innovation by introducing new and better products, keeping consumers interested. Warren Buffett looks for such companies that have dominated the market because of their unique offering and have the ability to sustain it for long time. Coca cola was one of the investments made by Warren Buffett because it had a durable competitive advantage over other beverage companies.

Warren Buffet invested in Coca Cola because it has a strong competitive advantage over other beverage companies. Coca Cola serve 8 billion 300 ml servings everyday around the world, if it charges one cent extra for each serving, it will generate extra revenue every day I am sure no one would mind paying a extra for one bottle of Coca Cola.

A durable competitive advantage not only helps a company in achieving better financial performance, it also prevents a company's business from being taken over by its peers by building an economic moat around itself. Let us understand what an economic moat is and how it is an advantage for a business.

Mediocre Business has Commodity-based firms, selling products in highly competitive markets in which price plays the key role in the purchase decision. Examples include oil and gas companies, the lumber industry, producers of raw food items such as corn and rice, etc. Buffett avoids commodity-based firms.

How do you spot a commodity-based company? Buffett looks for these characteristics:

- The firm has low profit margins (net income divided by sales).
- The firm has low return on equity (earnings per share divided by book value per share).
- Absence of any brand-name loyalty for its products.
- The presence of multiple producers.
- The existence of substantial excess capacity.
- Profits tend to be erratic.
- The firm's profitability depends upon management's ability to optimize the use of tangible assets.

Investor must look in a company key performance

"Time is a friend of the good business and the enemy of the mediocre". – Warren Buffett

Measures of Economic Performance

- Growth in revenues?
- Market share?
- Growth in Profits?
- Growth EPS?
- Profit Margin?
- Capital Efficiency?
- Return on Capital?

Solving relevant customer jobs and finding product-market fit is just one of many important factors that make up a business. Great technologies, products and services must also have the right business models to support and sustain them. You will fail even with value propositions that customers want or technologies that customers crave if your business model is flawed (e.g. few people know that Kodak, which filed for bankruptcy in 2012, helped invent the digital camera that crushed its business model).

The most obvious flaw is when a business model's value propositions generate more costs than revenues from customers. The business will inevitably disappear, even with the most successful value propositions. But it still happens all the time! You might pick the wrong revenue model or pricing structure or underestimate the costs you incur from the activities, resources, and partnerships required to create and deliver your value proposition.

Further, your business model is flawed if you fail to establish the proper channels to reach and deliver value to your customers. Does it matter how brilliant your value proposition is if your potential customers don't know about it or can't find it?

Your business model might also be flawed if you fail to establish customer relationships that allow you to successfully retain and grow your customer base sustainably (e.g. think Zynga or King and Candy Crush). Finally, your business model will fail if you focus on the wrong activities or lack access to the right key partners and resources to reliably create, deliver, and capture value long term.

Bad business models cheat customer as VW did.

Volkswagen, the world's second-biggest carmaker admitted that it has been dishonest with customers and regulators. It has installed a software in its cars that falsifies emissions data of its diesel cars. Unfortunately, it is a perfect example where the values promised to customers and the real behavior outright contradict. And because of the mismatch, Volkswagen is in a perfect storm.

Volkswagen faces a fines up to $18bn, criminal charges against its executives and legal actions from customers. At the same time a third of its market value was wiped out or the staggering amount of around €30bn.

The head of the US operations of Volkswagen admitted that they "totally screwed up". And I hope he meant the deed and not the disaster afterwards.

What happened? Volkswagen had to admit that 11 million of its diesel cars could be equipped with software to cheat on emission tests. The American Environmental Protection Agency (EPA) had accused the firm of faking pollution tests and thereby cheating on regulators, the public and customers.

The case is already bad enough, but what is even worse is that the deed and the behavior that lead to the deed totally contradicts what Volkswagen promises in its value proposition.

Volkswagen states in its brand three core messages of which one is: Responsible

According to the Webster, responsible means to be "able to choose for oneself between right and wrong"

Volkswagen always played the role of the company with high morals. Responsibility was their core value they wanted to pursue and used hefty in their marketing.

And cheating deliberately on emission test is just the opposite of being able to differentiate what is right or wrong. Cheating is wrong! And it is not cheating software but the whole behavior that let a whole company come up with a software to cheat. Dozens and more people at Volkswagen must have known this and did nothing against.

What does this tell us about the culture they have at the firm?

Unfortunately a lot.

And unfortunately, the car industry has a bad track record between their promises and reality when it comes to emission and fuel consumption. The car manufacturers promise low fuel consumption however, they can only be achieved in unrealistic test scenarios and not on the road. Actually, it's legal but totally against what Volkswagen promises to be responsible.

And as a responsible company you should live up to your standards and do not try to seek loopholes in regulation to mislead customers and the public. Still car companies do.

Kodak Decides to Press Pause on Digital Cameras

This is probably the most well-known of the world's worst business strategies. Yep - this is the story of how Kodak invented the digital camera, only to then decide not to launch one until over 15 years later!

In 1975, Steve Sasson created the world's first digital camera at the Kodak HQ in New York. It was a 0.1 Megapixel beast that was around the size of a toaster. It was also utterly revolutionary and would change the face of photography for ever. The team at Kodak were smart - and they knew just how big of a deal this was. So they invested millions of dollars into getting digital cameras into production. A few years later, they were all set to launch the world's first commercially available digital camera - until members of the senior management team put a stop to the whole endeavor.

Why? Because they were worried about hurting the performance of their film division - which relied on selling single-use rolls of films to customers with non-digital camera devices. Even when they were told that they had at most, 10 years until digital would completely displace film - they continued to resist in order to ensure that they met their own short term financial KPIs.

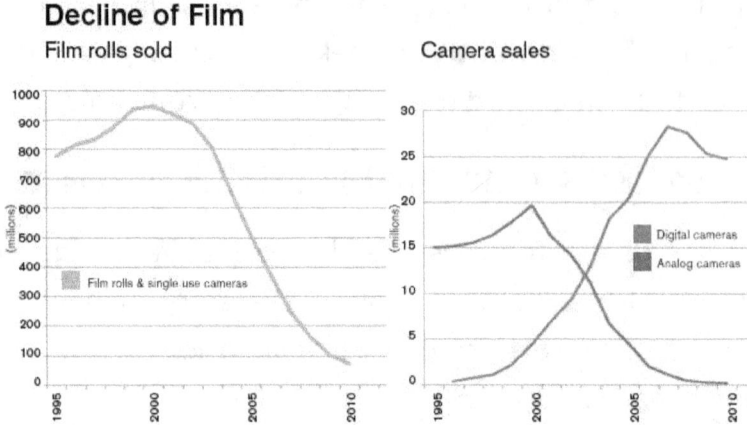

Decline of Film

Plenty of postmortems have been performed on Kodak's demise and how it implemented one of the world's worst business strategies. What most of them agree on is that key executives at the time were working far more towards short term profit goals than towards long term viability of the business.

Even though film sales were declining - the executives did a great job of managing the expectations of their shareholders down, so that bonuses were still being regularly paid out, even as sales continued to decline.

One of the models we often suggest to our clients to avoid this scenario, is to implement something like the McKinsey's Strategic Horizon model as part of your strategic plan. This model forces you to balance your goals between the 3 horizons of:

1: Revenue from business as usual (around 70% of your effort)

2: Focus on broadening your revenue streams (around 20 of your effort)

3: Focus on exploring entirely new revenue streams (around 10% of your effort)

Whilst this model might not have saved Kodak - it would at least have highlighted how little focus was being put on revenue streams beyond that of their traditional film business. Take a look at our guide to the best strategy frameworks for more information about McKinsey's Strategic Horizons.

It does not matter what amount of investment you are investing, it is far more important, and that you are selecting a right sustainable company that will grow in future.

Wrong Selection of the company by majority of investors:-

- Logo looks good so it must be good company.
- Mission and Vision statement look inspiring.
- A Big company, large market capital.
- Big market share.
- Branding to attract customer such as VW good branding and fraud management, Nissan and Renault good branding fraud management.
- Film Star Brand Ambassador.
- Management is in limelight.

Why Nokia Fail?

Nokia is the first brand that was in the market when we heard of the early mobile phones. For a decade, Nokia remained in the market and introduced new models of the phone every now and then. It catered all segments of society by providing the phone with different price ranges. Millennial would be able to relate with me better. With a glorifying history of the company, it gets hard to realize that Nokia is no more relevant in the mobile phone industry. But why Nokia failed?

Nokia emerged as one of the successful manufacturers of mobile phone in the early days of its success. In October 1998, Nokia was the best-selling mobile phone brand in the world. By 2007, it had 50% of the share from the mobile phone market. The young and energetic leadership of the company was the reason for its wide acceptance in the consumer market. Initially, the new technology, urge to digitalize and innovation were also amongst some of the reasons for success.

The technological advancement in the mobile phone industry was rapid. The traditional phones changed to smartphones, but Nokia did not change accordingly. Although, it was the initiator of the early smartphones. Symbian smartphones were introduced in the year 2002, but the company could not manage with the pace of the changing technology. That is why Nokia failed.

It kept on producing the old version of the phone, whereas the competitors started to pour in the highly advanced smartphones. These smartphones got affordable for the users, and ultimately, the entire cult of society shifted to them. Even then, Nokia did not realize what was going on and did not transform its strategies. Thus, over time, with the shifting of all its target market to a newer and better version of the phone took place, leaving Nokia far behind the new entrants of the market.

Gradually, the mobile phone industry became saturated with a lot of companies serving the same target market. Apple, Samsung, Blackberry, and Nokia all were the leading players striving for the target market. In this race of competition, Nokia did not improve its service and lost to the other players available in the market.

Historically chart of Mediocre Business

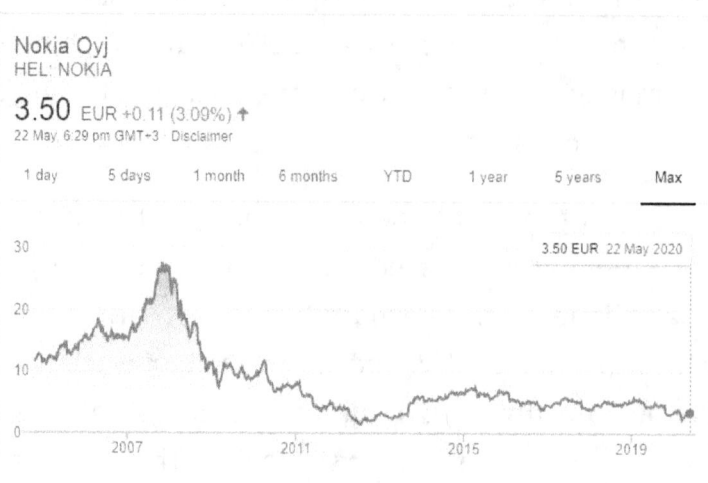

Nokia

Blackberry

General Motors Company
NYSE: GM

25.98 USD +0.18 (0.70%) ↑
Closed 22 May, 7:57 pm GMT-4 · Disclaimer
After hours 25.98 0.00 (0.00%)

GM

Eastman Kodak Company
NYSE: KODK

2.72 USD +0.060 (2.26%) ↑
22 May, 4:00 pm GMT-4 · Disclaimer

Kodak

Nissan

Renault

American Airlines Group

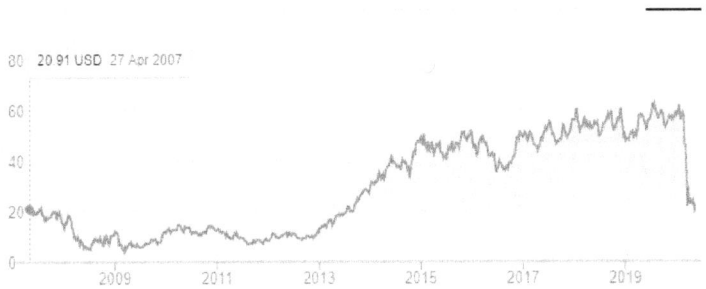

Delta Air Lines

Historically chart of Company having Competitive Advantage

Amazon

Apple Inc

Microsoft

Visa

Time is the friend of the wonderful business, the enemy of the mediocre.

By 1989, Warren Buffett was convinced that buying Berkshire Hathaway had been his first big mistake as an investor.

(By 2010, Buffett would say it was his biggest mistake ever — according to him, buying the company rather than insurance companies directly denied him returns of approximately $200B over the next 45 years.)

He bought Berkshire Hathaway because it was cheap. He knew that any temporary "hiccup" in the fortunes of the company would give him a good opportunity to offload the business for a profit.

The problem with that method, he reflects, is that mediocre companies (the kind that get offloaded for cheap in the first place) cost money in the time between you acquiring it and you selling it for a profit.

The approach of the more mature Buffett is to never invest in a company that can be a success if held for a short period of time. It is to only invest in companies that can succeed over an extremely long period of time, like 100 years or more.

"Time is the friend of the wonderful business, the enemy of the mediocre."

No business that is not generating value over the long-term is worth holding on to, and holding on to a bad business is never going to be a good investing strategy. This observation is important for Buffett, and for his overall conservative strategy in the market.

"The finding may seem unfair, but in both business and investments it is usually far more profitable to simply stick with the easy and obvious than it is to resolve the difficult," he writes.

This philosophy extends to how Buffett thinks about finding managers.

"Our goal is to attract long-term owners who, at the time of purchase, have no timetable or price target for sale but plan instead to stay with us indefinitely," he wrote in his 1988 letter, "We don't understand the CEO who wants lots of stock activity, for that can be achieved only if many of his owners are constantly exiting. At what other organization — school, club, church, etc. — do leaders cheer when members leave?"

Q&A

- What is business mediocrity? How it can affect your investment?
- Your Answer -

- In COVID 19 some company stock price is raising and some are bankrupt?
- Your Answer -

- In COVID 19 some company are not affected like other?
- Your Answer -

- In COVID 19 some companies like Wal-Mart make money and other like Renault failed?
- Your Answer -

- Why mediocre company cheat customer?
- Your Answer -

5

Timing the Market

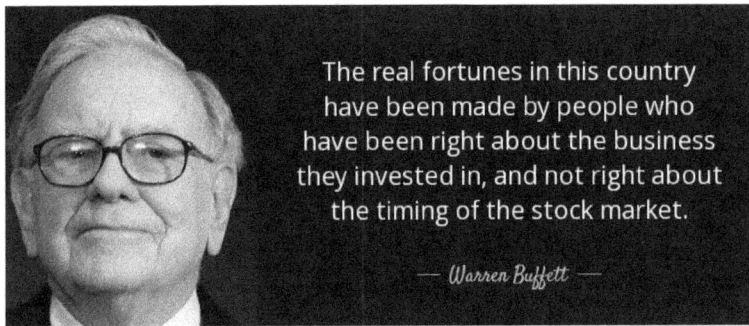

> The real fortunes in this country have been made by people who have been right about the business they invested in, and not right about the timing of the stock market.
>
> — *Warren Buffett*

Market timing is the strategy of making buying or selling decisions of financial assets (often stocks) by attempting to predict future market price movements. The prediction may be based on an outlook of market or economic conditions resulting from technical or fundamental analysis. This is an investment strategy based on the outlook for an aggregate market, rather than for a particular financial asset.

Whether market timing is ever a viable investment strategy is controversial. Some may consider market timing to be a form of gambling based on pure chance, because they do not believe in undervalued or overvalued markets. The efficient-market hypothesis claims that financial prices always exhibit random walk behavior and thus cannot be predicted with consistency.

Some consider market timing to be sensible in certain situations, such as an apparent bubble. However, because the economy is a complex system that contains many factors, even at times of significant market optimism or pessimism, it remains difficult, if not impossible, to predetermine the local maximum or minimum of future prices with any precision; a so-called bubble can last for many years before prices collapse. Likewise, a crash can persist for extended periods; stocks that appear to be "cheap" at a glance, can often become much cheaper afterwards, before then either rebounding at some time in the future or heading toward bankruptcy.

Proponents of market timing counter that market timing is just another name for trading. They argue that "attempting to predict future market price movements" is what all traders do, regardless of whether they trade individual stocks or collections of stocks, aka, mutual funds. Thus if market timing is not a viable investment strategy, the proponents say, and then neither is any of the trading on the various stock exchanges. Those who disagree with this view usually advocate a buy-and-hold strategy with periodic "re-balancing".

The Federal Reserve Bank of Kansas City has published a review of several relatively simple and statistically successful market-timing strategies. It found, for example, that "Extremely low spreads, as compared to their historical ranges, appear to predict higher frequencies of subsequent market downturns in monthly data" and that "the strategy based on the spread between the P/E ratio and a short-term interest rate comfortably and robustly beat the market index even when transaction costs are incorporated".

Institutional investors often use proprietary market-timing software developed internally that can be a trade secret. Some algorithms, like the one developed by Nobel Prize–winning economist Robert C. Merton, attempts to predict the future superiority of stocks versus bonds (or vice versa), have been published in peer-reviewed journals and are publicly accessible.

Above all the traders whoever predict the market, never made any money, they are not a billionaires.

Warren Buffett dealt with this situation in 1966. The Dow had a rough six months to start the year. It declined from 969.26 to 870.10.

I received a few calls from partners suggesting that they thought stocks were going a lot lower. This always raises two questions in my mind: (1) if they knew in February that the Dow was going to 865 in May, why didn't they let me in on it then; and, (2) if they didn't know what was going to happen during the ensuing three months back in February, how do they know in May? There is also a voice or two after any hundred point or so decline suggesting we sell and wait until the future is clearer. Let me again suggest two points: (1) the future has never been clear to me (give us a call when the next few months are obvious to you — or, for that matter the next few hours); and, (2) no one ever seems to call after the market has gone up one hundred points to focus my attention on how unclear everything is, even though the view back in February doesn't look so clear in retrospect.

If we start deciding, based on guesses or emotions, whether we will or won't participate in a business where we should have some long run edge, we're in trouble. We will not sell our interests in businesses (stocks) when they are attractively priced just because some astrologer thinks the quotations may go lower even though such forecasts are obviously going to be right some of the time. Similarly, we will not buy fully priced securities because "experts" think prices are going higher. Who would think of buying or selling a private business because of someone's guess on the stock market? The availability of a quotation for your business interest (stock) should always be an asset to be utilized if desired. If it gets silly enough in either direction, you take advantage of it. Its availability should never be turned into a liability whereby its periodic aberrations in turn formulate your judgments.

That's why Buffett avoids it:

We don't buy and sell stocks based upon what other people think the stock market is going to do (I never have an opinion) but rather upon what we think the company is going to do. The course of the stock market will determine, to a great degree, when we will be right, but the accuracy of our analysis of the company will largely determine whether we will be right. In other words, we tend to concentrate on what should happen, not when it should happen.

The Oracle of Omaha explained why investors should avoid market predictions during Berkshire Hathaway's annual shareholder meeting in 1994, obtained through the CNBC Warren Buffett archive.

"I never have an opinion about the market because it wouldn't be any good and it might interfere with the opinions we have that are good," Buffett said. "If we're right about a business, if we think a business is attractive, it would be very foolish for us to not take action on that because we thought something about what the market was going to do. ... If you're right about the businesses, you'll end up doing fine."

When there is a market crash generally investor asks this question is it a good time to buy stocks for the long term?

Right time to know where the treasure is hidden in stock market.

We wait for the years to buy best quality stock at attractive valuation and the company which have competitive advantage, strong moat and have margin of safety.

In the bull market it is not so easy to find the under value stock but when there is a collapse in the financial market, we are easily able to search for the hidden treasure, the quality stock, which meet our standard as per value investing.

First question the investor asked is that "Is it the right time to invest"? Or should we wait for more correction? The best we can do is to analyse the quality of the company and if we found that we have enough margin of safety, we should start investing.

Correction in the financial market is the indication to make enormous wealth, with no risk and to achieve good return. Currently the quality stocks are available at discounted price are Apple Inc @ $245, Bank of America @ $ 21,Visa Inc @ $165 , Johnson & Johnson @ $137 & Nike Inc @ $84 as on 22nd may 2020.

These are the best stock to buy and hold for a long time to create wealth. There is no right time to buy all we required is a margin of safety and sell at a high price at the right time. To buy at this current level, it is very safe, as we are facing such impact of coronavirus and due to this financial market is not performing.

Currently is a right time to construct the quality portfolio. The coronavirus can be worst as it look like and that will affect the financial system, in this case we should not be waiting for the right time, if we get the right valuation, we can buy at this level, as this virus gets controlled, then the market might need a year to get back on track and a good quality company can again be able to generate enough revenue and free cash flow.

Already we have seen the reaction of stock market due to coronavirus ,all the sectors have reacted differently , the majority of degrowth is seen in automobiles , & Aviation , Hospitality , Oil & Gas.

All sectors are not affected equally; the current market is processing different information and reacting differently.

Amazon Inc has gain 4% compare to S&P 500 YTD Return - 19.41%.

Best time to buy is when others are selling .Understanding the current market crisis; it is the right time to build a robust portfolio.

What we currently look in a company is the strong fundamental value. We should now focus on enough Margin of Safety rather than forecasting the earning or predicting where the market will be tomorrow .Due to low price, we can get margin of safety, a very good return in future and if the further price goes down, we should keep on buying.

It is the time to hunt for treasure at bargain price. We should not leave any stone unturned in creating quality Portfolio.

More important is right valuation and margin of safety, not the timing the market. At any given time you are buying stock at high valuation, your investment return will be less, the price and margin of safety determine your stock return not the timing.

Recent research from Dalbar Inc. found that the average investor earned a 5.19 percent return while the S&P 500 provided a 9.85 percent return over the same period. Investors underperform compared to the market thanks to emotional investing behavior, like buying when a stock price is high and overreacting to bad news.

"Buy high and sell low" is bad investment advice, but that is exactly what many irrational investors do when they enter trades based on the news and emotions. Knowing that others will make poor investment decisions, you can capture small profits when the markets overreact to market news.

"Far more money has been lost by investors trying to anticipate corrections, than lost in the corrections themselves."

-Peter Lynch

Invest need to Stay invested through all market environments and time will reward you for your patience.

Lesson from Peter Lynch

Talk about market timing.

The market itself is very volatile. We've had 95 years completed this century. We're in the middle of 1996 and we're close to a 10 percent decline. In the 95 years so far, we've had 53 declines in the market of 10 percent or more. Not 53 down years. The market might have been up 26 finished the year up four, and had a 10 percent correction. So we've had 53 declines in 95 years. That's once every two years. Of the 53, 15 of the 53 have been 25 percent or more. That's a bear market. So 15 in 95 years, about once every six years you're going to have a big decline. Now no one seems to know when there are gonna happen. At least if they know about 'em, they're not telling anybody about 'em. I don't remember anybody predicting the market right more than once, and they predict a lot. So they're gonna happen. If you're in the market, you have to know there's going to be declines. And they're going to cap and every couple of years you're going to get a 10 percent correction. That's a euphemism for losing a lot of money rapidly. That's what a "correction" is called. And a bear market is 20-25-30 percent decline. They're gonna happen. When they're gonna start, no one knows. If you're not ready for that, you shouldn't be in the stock market. I mean stomach is the key organ here. It's not the brain. Do you have the stomach for these kind of declines? And what's your timing like? Is your horizon one year? Is your horizon ten years or 20 years? If you've been lucky enough to save up lots of money and you're about to send one kid to college and your child's starting a year from now, you decide to invest in stocks directly or with a mutual fund with a one-year horizon or a two-year horizon, that's silly. That's just like betting on red or black at the casino. What the market's going to do in one or two years, you don't know. Time is on your side in the stock market. It's on your side. And when stocks go down, if you've got the money, you don't worry about it and you're putting more in, you shouldn't worry about it. You should worry what stocks are going to be 10 years from now, 20 years from now, 30 years from now. I'm very confident.

From Chapter 8 of The Intelligent Investor:

"By timing we mean the endeavor to anticipate the action of the stock market—to buy or hold when the future course is deemed to be upward, to sell or refrain from buying when the course is downward. By pricing we mean the endeavor to buy stocks when they are quoted below their fair value and to sell them when they rise above such value. A less ambitious form of pricing is the simple effort to make sure that when you buy you do not pay too much for your stocks. This may suffice for the defensive investor, whose emphasis is on long-pull holding; but as such it represents an essential minimum of attention to market levels.

We are convinced that the intelligent investor can derive satisfactory results from pricing of either type. We are equally sure that if he places his emphasis on timing, in the sense of forecasting, he will end up as a speculator and with a speculator's* financial results." - Benjamin Graham

Back in 2009, Warren Buffett said the following:

"We don't try to pick bottoms. To sit around and not do something sensible because you think there might be something better.... doesn't make sense. Picking bottoms is not our game. Pricing is our game. And that's not so difficult. Picking bottoms is, I think, impossible." - Warren Buffett

Buffett: Picking bottoms is impossible

Market participants attempting to get the timing right (something that seems more close to futile than not) end up distracted from what's important: Making price versus valuation judgments that, over the long haul, will get the best possible result at the least risk.

Attempts at timing is inherently speculative and a distraction away from the all-important price versus value discipline.

Mispriced assets often seem to get sorted out in nearly, if not completely, unpredictable ways in terms of timing. It's important to be realistic -- when the timing does happen to work out -- about the real reasons why. Successful moves don't always get the scrutiny they deserve.

Sometimes the favorable outcome was more about luck than great foresight.

Sometimes it has little to do with having some unusual talent for predicting the amount and timing of price movements.

Not knowing when a favorable outcome was mostly accidental is a recipe for future mistakes.

An approach dependent on lucky or accidental outcomes is destined to result in even bigger losses down the road if it leads to unwarranted overconfidence. A few successful outcomes resulting more from good fortune, less on real foresight, might encourage that market participant to put even larger amounts of capital at risk (with maybe less favorable outcomes). I'm not saying no one can effectively time these things (even though my interest in such an approach is effectively zero). I'm saying those that try had better have a realistic view of their own abilities.

Overestimation of one's own talent in this regard will likely end up being very expensive.

The good news is a long-term investor doesn't have to get the timing right if sound price versus value judgments are mostly being made. Mistakes are inevitable, of course. The key is keeping them small and infrequent. One way to keep them small and infrequent is to always pay an appropriate discount to a well-judged valuation. An appropriate margin of safety is protection against small misjudgments (since valuation even done well is inherently imprecise) and the unforeseen adverse developments that inevitably arise in an unpredictable world.

Developing competence when it comes to understanding how price relates to the value of an asset is a good use of energy.

Attempts at timing the market generally isn't.

Earlier in Chapter 8 Graham writes: "If you want to speculate do so with your eyes open, knowing that you will probably lose money in the end..."

Q&A

- **Timing to be a form of gambling?**
- Your Answer -

- **Right time to know where the treasure is hidden in stock market, what is state?**
- Your Answer -

- **What is margin of safety?**
- Your Answer -

- **Timing the market or company valuation is important?**
- Your Answer -

6

High Debt

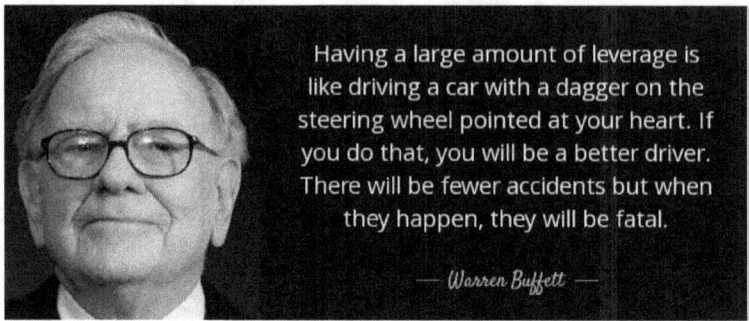

> Having a large amount of leverage is like driving a car with a dagger on the steering wheel pointed at your heart. If you do that, you will be a better driver. There will be fewer accidents but when they happen, they will be fatal.
>
> — Warren Buffett

When you invest in a company, you need to look at many different financial records to see if it is a worthwhile investment. But what does it mean to you if, after doing all your research, you invest in a company and then it decides to borrow money? Here we look at how you can evaluate whether the debt will affect your investment.

If a company has absolutely no debt, then taking on some debt may be beneficial because it can give the company more opportunity to reinvest resources into its operations. However, if the company in question already has a substantial amount of debt, you might want to think twice. Generally, too much debt is a bad thing for companies and shareholders because it inhibits a company's ability to create a cash surplus. Furthermore, high debt levels may negatively affect common stockholders, who are last in line for claiming payback from a company that becomes insolvent.

Loans and fixed-income securities that a company issues differ dramatically in their maturity dates. Some loans must be repaid within a few days of issue, while others don't need to be paid for several years. Typically, debt securities issued to the public (investors) will have longer maturities than the loans offered by private institutions (banks). Large short-term loans may be harder for companies to repay, but long-term fixed-income securities with high interest rates may not be easier on the company. Try to determine if the length and interest rate of the debt is suitable for financing the project that the company wishes to undertake.

A debt-to-equity ratio measures the amount of debt a company uses to fund its business for every dollar of equity it has. The ratio equals total liabilities divided by total stockholders' equity, which are found on the balance sheet. The higher the ratio is, the more debt a business uses compared to equity. A ratio that is too high can potentially cause problems in business.

Example

Business has $400,000 in total liabilities and $250,000 in total stockholders' equity, your debt-to-equity ratio is 1.6. This means you use $1.60 in debt for every $1 of equity, or your debt level is 160 percent of your equity.

It is one of the very important ratios to understand that investor should avoid such high debt company, unless you are very comfortable enough to know the reason why company have much debts, you should not buy the stock.

General Electric – Recent dividends paid to GE shareholders were roughly a single cent, with reported quarterly losses being over $22.8 billion. Excessive business debt plays a significant role in GE's, decline, which is roughly $115 million. Losing over 45% of the company's value this year, GE's debt-to-equity ratio is far from ideal. As a result, the company has to sell off numerous assets with hopes of restructuring its current debt situation.

Campbell Soup Company – As part of the acquisition wave, Campbell Soup borrowed $6 billion to purchase Snyder's Lance Inc. Unfortunately, this placed its business debt in excess of $10 billion. This naturally resulted in a markedly high debt-to-equity ratio for the company. And Campbell Soup's debt-to-earnings before interest, taxes, depreciation, and amortization (debt/EBITDA) was more than 5.0. As a result, the company now finds itself having to sell off longstanding valued assets in order to maintain operations.

Catalina Marketing – This former leader in coupon marketing strategies is trying to overcome a dying business model in an evolving marketplace. But in the process, Catalina Marketing has taken on more than $1.6 billion in debt while seeing its revenues progressively decline. The company's debt-to-earnings ratio is now higher than 12.0, which indicates a highly constrained financial environment. With such a high percentage of revenues going to pay off debt, opportunities for growth and revitalization are reduced. Since hiring turnaround specialist Gerald Sokol Jr. as President and CEO in October, it is rumored the company may be seeking chapter 11 bankruptcy protection, due to its debt and poor sales performance.

AT&T Inc. – This Texas-based conglomerate is the world's largest telecommunications company and a giant in the mobile phone sector. But despite AT&T's size and recent expansion – it acquired Time Warner – the company is saddled with roughly $190 billion in debt ($82 billion of which stems from the Time Warner deal). This debt load has put a damper on AT&T's growth outlook, along with its stock price and will continue to do so for some time.

An incorporated company files bankruptcy if the company is insolvent (i.e., its debts exceed its assets) and its shareholders (i.e., the company's owners) feel that the business cannot continue. A business usually cannot continue because it cannot pay its creditors in the normal course of business.

From an investor's point of view, there isn't much good to say about bankruptcy. No matter what type of investment you made in a company, once it goes bankrupt you are probably going to get less for your investment than you expected.

In general, Chapter 11 is better for investors than Chapter 7. But in either case, don't expect much. Relatively few companies undergoing Chapter 11 proceedings become profitable again after reorganization; even if they do, it is rarely a quick process. As an investor, you should react to a company's bankruptcy the same way you would if its shares took an unexpected dive for other reasons: Recognize the dramatically reduced prospects of the company and ask yourself whether you still want to be committed.

If the answer is no, let go of your failed investment. Holding on while the company undergoes bankruptcy proceedings may only lead to sleepless nights and perhaps even greater losses in the future. If nothing else, you may be able to take a capital loss on your taxes.

List of bankruptcies during the coronavirus pandemic

"As financial challenges continue to escalate amid this crisis, bankruptcy is sure to offer a financial safe harbor from the economic storm," the institute's executive director, Amy Quackenboss, said in a statement.

Companies that headed into this downturn without a financial cushion are already feeling the toll of the abrupt downturn. That's evident among retailers, which had been suffering from online competition and **high debt** prior to the pandemic. Retail sales tumbled 16.4% in April, with clothing stores taking this biggest hit.

Diamond Offshore Drilling

Prior to filing for bankruptcy, Diamond Offshore skipped an interest payment and secured restructuring advisers. The company also recently drew down $400 million under a revolving credit facility. Diamond Offshore currently has enough capital to continue normal operations as it undergoes restructuring efforts, according to a company statement.

Frontier Communications

The company expects its restructuring plan to reduce its debt by more than $10 billion. It also said it has received $460 million in debtor-in-possession financing. Combined with the company's more than $700 million in cash, the DIP financing will allow Frontier to have more than $1.1 billion in liquidity that will help it meet operational needs.

Gold's Gym

The fitness chain filed for bankruptcy on May 4 2020. Gold's Gym plans to permanently close around 30 company-owned gyms, but its franchised locations will reopen as coronavirus restrictions are lifted.

Intelsat

The company reported almost $15 billion in debt at the end of 2019, according to an SEC filing, and previously signaled trouble when it skipped a $125 million interest payment in April.

Ultra Petroleum

Ultra Petroleum previously warned of a potential filing in its fourth-quarter earnings release from April 14. On top of the company's approximately $2 billion in debt as of Dec. 31, Ultra Petroleum said in another SEC filing it faced "business disruption" from the coronavirus.

Through the restructuring agreement, Ultra Petroleum secured financing of up to $25 million and a revolving credit facility with an initial borrowing base of $100 million from lenders. The company said it will be able to eliminate $2 billion in debt.

Virgin Australia

Australia's second-biggest airline announced April 21 that it is undergoing third party-led restructuring that could potentially lead to a sale. The company currently has debt of AU$5 billion ($3.2 billion) and more than 10 parties have expressed interest in restructuring the company. Sir Richard Branson, founder of Virgin Group, a major shareholder of Virgin Australia, said in a tweet that his company would work to make Virgin Australia healthy again.

Hertz

The car rental company said there are doubts about its ability to continue as a going concern. It has secured debt restructuring advisers and is preparing for negotiations with creditors over its $17 billion in debt.

The car rental industry has taken serious blows from the coronavirus pandemic, and Hertz laid off 10,000 people amid the crisis, incurring employee termination costs of $30 million. Even before the outbreak, Hertz and other rental companies faced competition from rideshare companies like Uber.

JC Penney

The Plano, Texas-based company faces numerous challenges, including slumping sales and nearly $4 billion in debt. Most of J.C. Penney's stores have been closed since March 18 because of the coronavirus. The company decided to furlough most of its hourly workers starting April 2. Penney also recently had to go to court to keep makeup seller Sephora from pulling out of its stores.

The above example state that all those company who have debt cannot survive in the cycle time. The valuation any other matrix does not work out if the said company is in high debt and paying interest cost .

Debt Ratio = Total Liabilities / Total Assets

Total Liabilities are the total debt that the entity owns to others at the specific reporting date. The total liabilities could be found in the balance sheet or you can substrate the total equity from total assets to figure out total liabilities. The accounting equation could also use as the reference to calculated liabilities and assets from the balance sheet. Liabilities here included both current liabilities and non-current liabilities. That mean debt here included not only long term loan from banks, but also including account payable as well as prepayment from customers.

Total assets basically mean the control of the resources by the entity and will have future economic flow. In the balance sheet, total assets as the accumulation of both current and non-current assets. So, total assets including not only land, building, machinery, but also cash in banks, as well as cash on hand.

This ratio measures in percentages or time. In general, investors and bankers prefer the debt ratio smaller than one. The smaller the ratio, the good sign the entity could pay the bank the loan.

The debt-to-equity (D/E) ratio is a metric that provides insight into a company's use of debt. In general, a company with a high D/E ratio is considered a higher risk to lenders and investors because it suggests that the company is financing a significant amount of its potential growth through borrowing. What is considered a high ratio can depend on a variety of factors, including the company's industry.

Raising debt is like playing Russian roulette by Warren Buffett.

All across the business world, from big, corporate boardrooms to the offices of venture capitalists, managers employ the use of debt to juice returns. Whether it's a company like Uber taking on $1.5B to re-energize its slowing growth or a startup like ModCloth taking on $20M to find that initial growth curve, debt offers companies a way to acquire capital without giving up room on their cap table or diluting existing shares.

Debt also forces shareholders into a Russian roulette equation, according to Buffett in his 2018 letter. And "a Russian roulette equation — usually win, occasionally die — may make financial sense for someone who gets a piece of a company's upside but does not share in its downside. But that strategy would be madness for Berkshire," he writes.

Because of the incentive structure involved, the venture capital model where one great success of an investment can cover the losses of a hundred failures is especially prone to recommending the use of debt.

A stock speculator is equally likely to promote the use of debt to increase returns because they can build out portfolios where they don't have to worry about the downside risk. For them, it can make good sense to do so, since as Buffett points out, they're usually not going to get a "bullet" when they pull the "trigger."

For Buffett, however, who owns so many companies outright and intends to continue holding them for the long-term, an outcome of "usually win, occasionally die" doesn't make sense.

The risk of a company failing and a significant amount of debt getting called back is too great a risk, and Buffett and Berkshire Hathaway share in that risk equally with their shareholders.

Berkshire utilizes debt, but primarily through its railroad and utility subsidiaries. For these extremely asset-laden businesses that have constant equipment and capital needs, debt makes more sense, and they will generate plentiful amounts of cash for Berkshire Hathaway even in an economic downturn.

Borrow money when it's cheap

The Oracle of Omaha's famous cost-consciousness does not mean that Berkshire Hathaway never borrowed money or went into debt — on the contrary, Buffett makes clear in his letters that he is enthusiastic about borrowing money in one type of circumstance.

Buffett is an advocate of borrowing money at a modest rate when he believes it is both "properly structured" and "of significant benefit to shareholders." In reality, that usually means when economic conditions are tight and liabilities are expensive.

"We borrow… because we think that, over a period far shorter than the life of the loan, we will have many opportunities to put that money to good use," Buffett writes, "The most attractive opportunities may present themselves at a time when credit is extremely expensive — or even unavailable. At such a time, we want to have plenty of financial firepower."

When money is expensive, having more of it (in the form of debt) is a way of setting yourself up to take full advantage of opportunities. This fits nicely into Buffett's general investment worldview that the best time to buy is when everyone is selling.

"Tight money conditions, which translate into high costs for liabilities, will create the best opportunities for acquisitions, and cheap money will cause assets to be bid to the sky. Our conclusion: Action on the liability side should sometimes be taken independent of any action on the asset side."

Never use borrowed money to buy stocks

If there's a practice that infuriates Warren Buffett more than poorly structured executive compensation plans, it is going into debt to buy stocks or excessively finance acquisitions.

Much of Berkshire's early success came down to the intelligent use of leverage on relatively cheap stocks, as a 2013 study from AQR Capital Management and Copenhagen Business School showed. But Buffett's main problem is not with the concept of debt — it is with the type of high-interest, variable-rate debt that consumer investors must take on if they want to use it to buy stocks.

When ordinary people borrow money to buy stocks, they're putting their livelihoods in the hands of a market whose swings can be random and violent, even when it comes to a reliable stock like Berkshire's. In doing so, they risk potentially losing much more than their initial investment.

When a stock falls by more than 37%, a highly-leveraged investor stands a fair chance of incurring a margin call, where their broker calls and asks them to deposit more money in their account or risk having the rest of their securities portfolio liquidated to cover the losses.

"We believe it is insane to risk what you have and need in order to obtain what you don't need," Buffett writes. That's why Buffett is a fan of some kinds of debt, just not the kind that can leave consumers broke when the market swings down.

Q&A

- **Due to high Debt Company become insolvent?**
- **Your Answer -**

- High Debt Company creates value to the shareholders?
- Your Answer -

- Investing in a High Debt company is a high risk investment ?
- Your Answer -

- High Debts = Total Liabilities /Total Assets?
- Your Answer -

- Debt Ratio is 200, it is high or low?
- Your Answer

7

Forecast

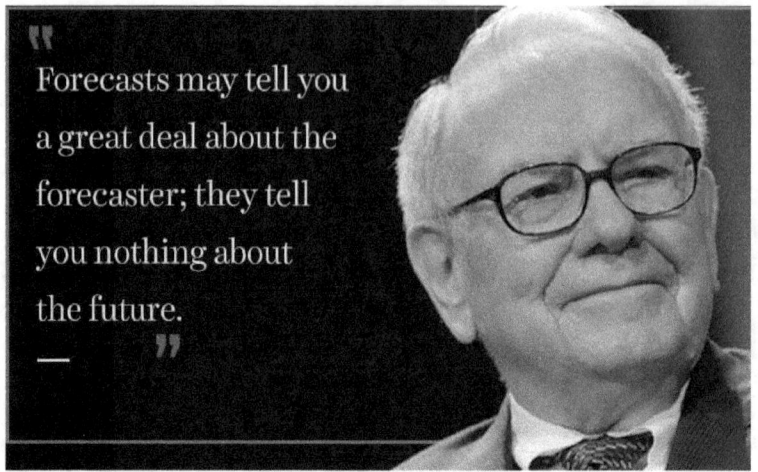

> Forecasts may tell you a great deal about the forecaster; they tell you nothing about the future.

Wall Street is the place where investor only forecast, what will be the earning? What will be the free cash flow? What will be price of the stock after six month? Investor needs to understand the business; how business works rather than forecasting, forecasting will never make you a millionaire, investor waste so much time in forecasting, finally desired result never comes.

It is better investor use the investment checklist to understand the business, Checklist investing is a simple process with tremendous benefits. An investment checklist can protect you from yourself, and propel you towards investment success.

Investors can benefit from outsourcing their discipline to an investment checklist in the way pilots do. Pilots use checklists prior to take-off to make sure everything is functioning as it should, and investors can use a checklist to make sure all is in order prior to investment.

Checklists are great for reducing human error, but they are also valuable in that they provide a type of documentation. Imagine one follows the checklist prior to investing in stocks and it doesn't work out. A smart, motivated investor can examine what went wrong and see if another item needs to be added to the investment checklist.

Investor and analyst do Economic forecasting is the process of making predictions about the economy. Forecasts can be carried out at a high level of aggregation—for example for GDP, inflation, unemployment or the fiscal deficit—or at a more disaggregated level, for specific sectors of the economy or even specific firms.

Many institutions engage in economic forecasting: national governments, banks and central banks, consultants and private sector entities such as think-tanks, companies and international organizations such as the International Monetary Fund, World Bank and the OECD. Some forecasts are produced annually, but many are updated more frequently.

The economist typically considers risks (i.e., events or conditions that can cause the result to vary from their initial estimates). These risks help illustrate the reasoning process used in arriving at the final forecast numbers. Economists typically use commentary along with data visualization tools such as tables and charts to communicate their forecast. In preparing economic forecasts a variety of information has been used in an attempt to increase the accuracy.

Investors utilize forecasting to determine if events affecting a company, such as sales expectations, will increase or decrease the price of shares in that company. Forecasting also provides an important benchmark for firms, which need a long-term perspective of operations.

Stock analysts use forecasting to extrapolate how trends, such as GDP or unemployment, will change in the coming quarter or year. The further out the forecast, the higher the chance that the estimate will be inaccurate. Finally, statisticians utilize forecasting in any situation that requires the use of forecasting. For instance, data may be collected regarding the impact of customer satisfaction by changing business hours or the productivity of employees upon changing certain work conditions.

Forecasting addresses a problem or set of data. Economists make assumptions regarding the situation being analyzed that must be established before the variables of the forecasting are determined. Based on the items determined, an appropriate data set is selected and used in the manipulation of information. The data is analyzed, and the forecast is determined. Finally, a verification period occurs where the forecast is compared to the actual results to establish a more accurate model for forecasting in the future.

The COVID-19 outbreak around world has never been predicted based on the pattern of china .No one using number churching. What happened to whose investor or analyst predicted the stock price will increase and suddenly due to COVID -19 stock market crashes? If you are predicting the stock price, you are wasting your precious time, its better you should read about company five years annual report.

A very common practice by analyst and investor Stock market prediction is the act of trying to determine the future value of a company stock or other financial instrument traded on an exchange. The successful prediction of a stock's future price could yield significant profit. The efficient-market hypothesis suggests that stock prices reflect all currently available information and any price changes that are not based on newly revealed information thus are inherently unpredictable. Others disagree and those with this viewpoint possess myriad methods and technologies which purportedly allow them to gain future price information. Value investor avoids this kind of approach.

Warren Buffett Long-term stock forecast

"Forecasting interest rates has never been our game, and Charlie and I have no idea what rates will average over the next year, or ten or thirty years. Our perhaps jaundiced view is that the pundits who opine on these subjects reveal, by that very behavior, far more about themselves than they reveal about the future. What we can say is that if something close to current rates should prevail over the coming decades and if corporate tax rates also remain near the low level businesses now enjoy, it is almost certain that equities will over time perform far better than long-term, fixed-rate debt instruments. That rosy prediction comes with a warning: Anything can happen to stock prices tomorrow. Occasionally, there will be major drops in the market, perhaps of 50% magnitude or even greater. But the combination of The American Tailwind, about which I wrote last year, and the compounding wonders described by Mr. Smith, will make equities the much better long-term choice for the individual who does not use borrowed money and who can control his or her emotions. Others? Beware!"

Pay attention to company earnings, not quarter-by-quarter stock gains

"Charlie and I urge you to focus on operating earnings – which were little changed in 2019 – and to ignore both quarterly and annual gains or losses from investments, whether these are realized or unrealized.

Buy stock as an owner, not a speculator

When many investors buy stock, they become price-obsessed, constantly checking the ticker to see if they're up or down money on any given day.

From Buffett's perspective, buying a stock should follow the same kind of rigorous analysis as buying a business. "If you aren't willing to own a stock for ten years, don't even think about owning it for ten minutes," he wrote in his 1996 letter.

Rather than getting too caught up in the price or recent movement of a stock, Buffett says, buy from companies that make great products, that have strong competitive advantages, and that can provide you with consistent returns over the long-term.

In short, buy stock in businesses that you would like to own yourself.

"Whenever Charlie and I buy common stocks for Berkshire's insurance companies... we approach the transaction as if we were buying into a private business," he wrote in his 1987 letter, "We look at the economic prospects of the business, the people in charge of running it, and the price we must pay. We do not have in mind any time or price for sale."

Take his investment in (and later acquisition of) the auto insurer GEICO — an acquisition that has been called Buffett's best ever.

GEICO represented everything Buffett was looking for as an investor. It had a great brand. It had a strong management team that he trusted. And when he first visited the company's headquarters in 1951, he saw "the huge cost advantage the company enjoyed over the giants of the industry." The combination of all these factors "set his heart afire."

In 1951, Buffett made the decision to invest more half of his net worth in GEICO. He increased his holdings dramatically during the bear market of the mid-70s when GEICO was struggling. By 1995, he owned half of the company — and later that year, he arranged to buy the rest.

"We agreed to pay $2.3 billion for the half of the company we didn't own. That is a steep price. But it gives us full ownership of a growing enterprise whose business remains exceptional for precisely the same reasons that prevailed in 1951," Buffett wrote in his 1995 letter.

Perhaps no other investment better represents Buffett's ideal as this 50-year investment in GEICO.

Buffett concedes that those who invest in companies on the speculation that they may one day be worthwhile could reap returns — he just has no interest in that kind of investment. He prefers to invest in companies that are already successful (even if that success is undervalued by the market) and that have a strong chance of continuing success over the long term.

That conviction gives him the ability to buy even bigger portions of the companies in which he invests when the overall market goes into a downturn. With a speculator mentality, Buffett might have offloaded GEICO's stock in the mid-70's. With a downturn in progress and healthy gains already realized, he would have come out ahead. With his owner mentality, however, Buffett used the downturn as an opportunity to amass an even greater share of the company.

In 2013, Buffett reported that GEICO had generated $73B for Berkshire Hathaway in one year — not a bad single-year return for a company that Buffett took over for $2.3B.

Financial forecast

A financial forecast is an estimate of future financial outcomes for a company. Financial forecasts estimate future income and expenses for a business over a period of time, generally the next year. They are used to develop projections for profit and loss statements, balance sheets, burn rate, and other cash flow forecasts.

Financial forecasts can use historical accounting and sales data, and external market and economic indicators, to predict what will happen to the company in financial terms over the given period of time.

Many investor use different approaches to predict the market , the stock price , Stock market prediction is the act of trying to determine the future value of a company stock or other financial instrument traded on an exchange. The successful prediction of a stock's future price could yield significant profit; does it make investor billionaire like Warren Buffett? The answer is no.

Investor use different tools to forecast such as:-

- To predict stock market investor seeks friends, to take tips.

- Investor seeks Astrologer to predict stock price.

- The PSO algorithm is employed to optimize LS-SVM to predict the daily stock prices. Proposed model is based on the study of stocks historical data and technical indicators. PSO algorithm selects best free parameters combination for LS-SVM to avoid over-fitting and local minima problems and improve prediction accuracy.

- Tips from expert, featuring on Tv.

- Using Python & Linear Regression.

The Agency Problem

The agency problem is a conflict of interest inherent in any relationship where one party is expected to act in another's best interests. In corporate finance, the agency problem usually refers to a conflict of interest between a company's management and the company's stockholders. The manager, acting as the agent for the shareholders, or principals, is supposed to make decisions that will maximize shareholder wealth even though it is in the manager's best interest to maximize his own wealth.

Regulations

Principle-agent relationships can be regulated, and often are, by contracts, or laws in the case of fiduciary settings. The Fiduciary Rule is an example of an attempt to regulate the arising agency problem in the relationship between financial advisors and their clients. The term fiduciary in the investment advisory world means that financial and retirement advisors are to act in the best interests of their clients. In other words, advisors are to put their clients' interests above their own. The goal is to protect investors from advisors who are concealing any potential conflict of interest.

For example, an advisor might have several investment funds that are available to offer a client, but instead only offers the ones that pay the advisor a commission for the sale. The conflict of interest is an agency problem whereby the financial incentive offered by the investment fund prevents the advisor from working on behalf of the client's best interest.

__Charlie Munger on projections__

Usually, I don't use formal projections. I don't let people do them for me because I don't like throwing up on the desk (laughter), but I see them made in a very foolish way all the time, and many people believe in them, no matter how foolish they are. It's an effective sales technique in America to put a foolish projection on a desk.

And if you're an investment banker, it's an art form. I don't read their projections either. Once Warren and I bought a company and the seller had a big study done by an investment banker, it was about this thick. We just turned it over as if it were a diseased carcass. He said, "We paid $2 million for that." I said, "We don't use them. Never look at them."

"You don't need higher math in business and if you learn it you feel tempted to use it – to your detriment. You really have to understand the company and its competitive positions; that's not disclosed by the math. There is something to be said for 'keeping it simple.'"

"Some of the worst business decisions I've seen are those that are done with a lot of formal projections and discounts back. And the trouble with that approach is that you get to believing the figures. And it seems that higher mathematics with more false precision should help you, but it doesn't."

"People have always had this craving to have someone tell them the future. Long ago, kings would hire people to read sheep guts. There's always been a market for people who pretend to know the future. Listening to today's forecasters is just as crazy as when the king hired the guy to look at the sheep guts. It happens over and over and over."

"Macroeconomics people are often wrong because of extreme complexity in the system they wish to understand. The trouble with making all these macroeconomic predictions is that people start to think they know something. It's much better to just say you're ignorant."

We've long felt that the only value of stock forecasters is to make fortune tellers look good. Even now, Charlie Munger and I continue to believe that short-term market forecasts are poison and should be kept locked up in a safe place, away from children and also from grown-ups who behave in the market like children.

"Every year I talk to the executives of a thousand companies, and I can't avoid hearing from the various gold bugs, interest rate disciples, Federal Reserve watchers, and fiscal mystics quoted in the newspapers. Thousands of experts study overbought indicators, oversold indicators, head and shoulder patters, put-call ratios, the Fed's policy on money supply, foreign investment, movement of all the constellations through the heavens, and the moss on the oak trees and they can't predict markets with any useful consistency any more than the gizzard squeezers could tell the Roman emperors when the Huns would attack."

Peter Lynch

"I don't know how to predict the stock market, I don't know how to predict interest rates, I don't know how to predict business. All I know is if I buy the right kind of business at the right price with the right people I'll do well over time. In stocks it's very hard to know when something will happen and it's very easy to know what will happen"

Warren Buffett

Q&A

- **Forecasting is a way to understand business?**
- **Your Answer - True or False**

- **It is better to use the investment checklist to understand the business?**
- **Your Answer - True or False**

- **Have any analyst or investor predicted Covid 19 market crash?**

- Your Answer -

- Buy stock as an owner, not a speculator?
- Your Answer -

- You want to be an Astrologer or a Successful Investor?
- Your Answer -

8

Corporate Governance

Corporate governance is the system of rules, practices, and processes by which a firm is directed and controlled. Corporate governance essentially involves balancing the interests of a company's many stakeholders, such as shareholders, senior management executives, customers, suppliers, financiers, the government, and the community. Since corporate governance also provides the framework for attaining a company's objectives, it encompasses practically every sphere of management, from action plans and internal controls to performance measurement and corporate disclosure.

A company's corporate governance is important to investors since it shows a company's direction and business integrity. Good corporate governance helps companies build trust with investors and the community. As a result, corporate governance helps promote financial viability by creating a long-term investment opportunity for market participants.

While corporate governance structure may vary, most organizations incorporate the following key elements:

- All shareholders should be treated equally and fairly. Part of this is making sure shareholders are aware of their rights and how to exercise them.
- Legal, contractual and social obligations to non-shareholder stakeholders must be upheld. This includes always communicating pertinent information to employees, investors, vendors and members of the community.
- The board of directors must maintain a commitment to ensure accountability, fairness, diversity and transparency within corporate governance. Board members must also possess the adequate skills necessary to review management practices.
- Organizations should define a code of conduct for board members and executives, only appointing new individuals if they meet that standard.
- All corporate governance policies and procedures should be transparent or disclosed to relevant stakeholders.

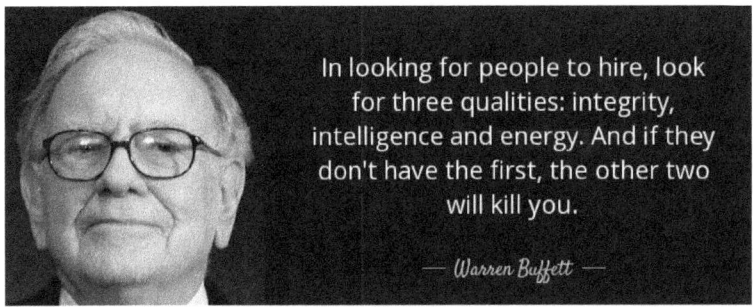

Integrity is the practice of being honest and showing a consistent and uncompromising adherence to strong moral and ethical principles and values. In ethics, integrity is regarded as the honesty and truthfulness or accuracy of one's actions. Integrity can stand in opposition to hypocrisy, in that judging with the standards of integrity involves regarding internal consistency as a virtue, and suggests that parties holding within themselves apparently conflicting values should account for the discrepancy or alter their beliefs. The word integrity evolved from the Latin adjective integer, meaning whole or complete. In this context, integrity is the inner sense of "wholeness" deriving from qualities such as honesty and consistency of character. As such, one may judge that others "have integrity" to the extent that they act according to the values, beliefs and principles they claim to hold.

Billionaire Warren Buffett, CEO of Berkshire Hathaway, understood this premise by calling integrity the most important hiring trait you want in an employee. Buffett said:

"We look for three things when we hire people. We look for intelligence, we look for initiative or energy, and we look for integrity. And if they don't have the latter, the first two will kill you, because if you're going to get someone without integrity, you want them lazy and dumb."

It was Charlie Munger (Buffett's longtime friend and co-investor) who convinced him otherwise:

Munger encouraged Buffett to adopt a long-term view of business opportunities, rather than the approach of bargain hunting Buffett had practiced in his early career. Munger [factored] in not only statistical analysis of balance sheet quantities and earnings, but soft factors like entrepreneurship, integrity, and reputation.

Buffett is not only willing to pay a premium for companies he sees as having more integrity, but also to maintain his own good reputation in the business community, as a takeover bid from the 1970s shows.

Warren Buffett breaks down why those three qualities – integrity, intelligence, and energy – are so important:

Play one game a little bit with me for just a minute…

I'd like for the moment to have you pretend I've made you a great offer, and I've told you that you could pick any one of your classmates – and you now know each other probably pretty well after being here for a while. You have 24 hours to think it over and you can pick any one of your classmates, and you get 10 percent of their earnings for the rest of their lives. And I ask you, what goes through your mind in determining which one of those you would pick? You can't pick the one with the richest father, that doesn't count. I mean, you've got to do this on merit. But, you probably wouldn't pick the person that gets the highest grades in the class.

I mean, there's nothing wrong with getting the highest grades in the class, but that isn't going to be the quality that sets apart a big winner from the rest of the pack. Think about who you would pick and why. And I think you'll find when you get through, you'll pick some individual – you've all got the ability, you wouldn't be here otherwise. And you've all got the energy. I mean, the initiative is here, the intelligence is here throughout the class. But some of you are going to be bigger winners than others.

And it gets down to a bunch of qualities that, interestingly enough, are self-made. I mean it's not how tall you are. It's not whether you can kick a football 60 yards. It's not whether you can run the 100 yard dash in 10 seconds. It's not whether you're the best looking person in the room. It's a whole bunch of qualities that really come out of Ben Franklin, or the Boy Scout codes, or whatever it may be. I mean, it's integrity, it's honesty, it's generosity, it's being willing to do more than your share, it's just all those qualities that are self-selected.

And then if you look on the other side of the ledger, because there's always a catch to these free gifts and genie jokes. So, you also have to – and this is the fun part – you also have to sell short one of your classmates and pay 10 percent of what they do. So, who do you think is going to do the worst in the class? This is way more fun. And think about it again. And again, it isn't the person with the lowest grades or anything of the sort. It's the person who just doesn't shape up in the character department.

We look for three things when we hire people. We look for intelligence, we look for initiative or energy, and we look for integrity. And if they don't have the latter, the first two will kill you, because if you're going to get someone without integrity, you want them lazy and dumb. I mean, you don't want a spark of energy out of them. So it's that third quality. But everything about that quality is your choice.

You know, you can't change the way you were wired much, but you can change a lot of what you do with that wiring. And it's the habits that you generate now on those qualities, or those negatives qualities. I mean the person who always claims credit for things they didn't do, that always cuts corners, that you can't count on. In the end those are habit patterns, and the time to form the right habits is when you're your age. I mean it doesn't do me much good to get golf lessons now. If I'd gotten golf lessons when I was your age I might be a decent golfer.

But, someone once said "the chains of habit are too light to be felt until they're too heavy to be broken." And I see that all the time. I see people with habit patterns that are self-destructive when they're 50 or 60 and they really can't change then, they're imprisoned by them. But you're not imprisoned by anything. So, when you write down the qualities of that person that you'd like to buy 10 percent of, look at that list and ask yourself, is there anything on that list I couldn't do?

And the answer is there won't be. And when you look at the person you sell short, and you look at those qualities that you don't like, if you see any of those in yourself – egotism, whatever it may be, selfishness – you can get rid of that. That is not ordained. And if you follow that, and Ben Franklin did this and my old boss Ben Graham did this at early ages in their young teens, Ben Graham looked around and he said, "Who do I admire?" And he wanted to be admired himself and he said, "Why do I admire these other people?" And he said, "If I admire them for these reasons, maybe other people would admire me if I behave in a similar manner." And he decided what kind of a person he wanted to be.

And if you follow that, at the end you'll be the person you want to buy 10 percent of. I mean that's the goal in the end, and it's something that's achievable by everybody in this room. So that's the end of the sermon.

Bad Corporate Governance

Bad corporate governance can cast doubt on a company's reliability, integrity, or obligation to shareholders—all of which can have implications on the firm's financial health. Tolerance or support of illegal activities can create scandals like the one that rocked Volkswagen AG starting in September 2015. The development of the details of "Dieselgate" (as the affair came to be known) revealed that for years, the automaker had deliberately and systematically rigged engine emission equipment in its cars in order to manipulate pollution test results, in America and Europe. Volkswagen saw its stock shed nearly half its value in the days following the start of the scandal, and its global sales in the first full month following the news fell 4.5%.

Public and government concern about corporate governance tends to wax and wane. Often, however, highly publicized revelations of corporate malfeasance revive interest in the subject. For example, corporate governance became a pressing issue in the United States at the turn of the 21st century, after fraudulent practices bankrupted high-profile companies such as Enron and WorldCom. It resulted in the 2002 passage of the Sarbanes-Oxley Act, which imposed more stringent recordkeeping requirements on companies, along with stiff criminal penalties for violating them and other securities laws. The aim was to restore public confidence in public companies and how they operate.

Other types of bad governance practices include:

- Companies do not cooperate sufficiently with auditors or do not select auditors with the appropriate scale, resulting in the publication of spurious or noncompliant financial documents.
- Bad executive compensation packages fail to create an optimal incentive for corporate officers.
- Poorly structured boards make it too difficult for shareholders to ineffective incumbents.

Theranos

In the approximately 15 years Theranos was in operation, the health technology company was able to raise more than

$700 million in venture capital and reach a peak valuation of $10 billion without publishing a single scientific research paper. The company was led by founder Elizabeth Holmes, who started Theranos at age 19 and was a frequent subject of praise by media outlets like The New Yorker, Forbes, and Fortune.

The company touted technology that could perform a wide range of lab tests with a single drop of blood, but an October 2015 expose in The Wall Street Journal claimed Theranos had deceived the public. This opened the company to further scrutiny. The fallout began shortly thereafter, and Holmes was charged with massive fraud in March 2018. The former wunderkind is currently set to stand trial in federal court in 2020 and will face penalties of up to 20 years in prison and tens of millions of dollars in fines.

Turing Pharmaceuticals HIV drug price gouging

Former Turing Pharmaceuticals CEO Martin Shkreli in 2015 increased the cost of the life saving drug Daraprim by 5,000%, driving the price of the drug from $13.50 to $750 per pill. Daraprim, which costs less than a dollar to manufacture, is a medicine for toxoplasmosis, which can lead to deadly infections in people with HIV and affects about 2,000 Americans per year. The price hike caused widespread outrage. Shkreli was required to testify in front of Congress over the company's pricing tactics and was eventually convicted in an unrelated case of securities fraud for which he is currently serving a seven-year prison sentence.

The Martin Shkreli scandal was big news on its own but was by no means an isolated problems throughout the decade.

To give just one example, it was just one year later that pharmaceutical company Mylan boosted prices by 400% for its EpiPen auto injector, a life saving medicine for cases of severe allergic reactions.

Wells Fargo account fraud

The Consumer Financial Protection Bureau revealed on Sept. 8, 2016, that Wells Fargo employees had opened more than 2 million unauthorized deposit and credit card accounts. In order to reach sales targets and other incentives, thousands of employees had opened accounts without customer consent. They also transferred funds from authorized accounts into the unauthorized accounts, which racked up fees and other charges for the unsuspecting customers.

Wells Fargo has been hit with over $2 billion in penalties related to the phony accounts since the scandal broke. Over 5,000 employees were fired in connection with the fake accounts, and CEO John Stumpf was forced to retire. Credit card applications plummeted in October 2016, and the Better Business Bureau revoked its accreditation of the bank.

Equifax data breach

Credit reporting agency Equifax announced on Sept. 7, 2017, that an unauthorized third party had gained access to the information of up to 143 million Americans — roughly half the U.S. population. According to a report published in Vice, Equifax may have known about the vulnerability from a security researcher's warning, but failed to act on it. Information contained in the files accessed by hackers included names, dates of birth, Social Security numbers, addresses, and, in about 209,000 cases, credit card numbers.

While the breach led to widespread public outrage, consumers were further incensed by the poor response to the incident. Equifax provided little explanation of the breach, and cybersecurity experts noted that the website Equifax directed customers to learn if their information was compromised was itself a security risk. The site also contained terms of use that, according to some lawyers, may have waived the customer's right to a class action lawsuit.

Boeing 737 MAX back-to-back plane crashes

On Oct. 29, 2018, a Lion Air flight departing from Indonesia crashed into the sea just moments after takeoff, killing all 189 people on board. Several months later, on March 10, 2019, an Ethiopian Airlines flight crashed shortly after takeoff, killing all 157 people on board. The planes involved in both accidents were Boeing 737 Max jets.

Shortly after the second crash, aviation authorities around the world grounded the 737 Max jet. Boeing ceased production of the aircraft, and is now the subject of several federal investigations and lawsuits. The lawsuit alleges Boeing had foreknowledge of the issue, which was partly what prompted the investigation and contributed to the public outrage. As of December 2019, Boeing has paid more than $9 billion in customer compensation costs related to the halted production. In the second quarter of 2019, Boeing posted a net loss of $2.9 billion, the largest quarterly loss in the company's history, as the company took a $4.9 billion related to the jet.

Bernard Madoff (2008)

Bernard Madoff, the former chairman of the Nasdaq and founder of the market-making firm Bernard L. Madoff Investment Securities, was turned in by his two sons and arrested on Dec. 11, 2008, for allegedly running a Ponzi scheme. The 70-year-old kept his hedge fund losses hidden by paying early investors with money raised from others. This fund consistently recorded an 11% gain every year for 15 years. The fund's supposed strategy, which was provided as the reason for these consistent returns, was to use proprietary option collars that are meant to minimize volatility. This scheme duped investors out of approximately $50 billion.

HealthSouth (2003)

Accounting for large corporations can be a difficult task, particularly when executives want to falsify earnings reports. In the late 1990s, CEO and founder Richard Scrushy began instructing employees to inflate revenues and overstate HealthSouth's net income. At the time, the company was one of America's largest health care service providers, experiencing rapid growth and acquiring a number of other healthcare-related firms. The first sign of trouble surfaced in late 2002 when Scrushy reportedly sold HealthSouth shares worth $75 million prior to releasing an earnings loss. An independent law firm concluded the sale was not directly related to the loss, and investors should have heeded the warning.

The scandal unfolded in March 2003, when the SEC announced that HealthSouth exaggerated revenues by $1.4

billion. The information came to light when CFO William Owens, working with the FBI, taped Scrushy discussing the fraud. The repercussions were swift as the stock fell from a high of $20 to a close of 45 cents in a single day. Amazingly, the CEO was acquitted of 36 counts of fraud but was later convicted on charges of bribery. Apparently, Scrushy arranged political contributions of $500,000, allowing him to ensure a seat on the hospital regulatory board.

WorldCom Scandal (2002)

WorldCom was an American telecommunications company based out of Ashburn, Virginia. In 2002, just a year after the Enron scandal, it was discovered that WorldCom had inflated its assets by almost $11 billion, making it by far one of the largest accounting scandals ever.

The company had underreported line costs by capitalizing instead of expensing them and had inflated its revenues by making false entries. The scandal first came to light when the company's internal audit department found almost $3.8 billion in fraudulent accounts. The company's CEO, Bernie Ebbers, was sentenced to 25 years in prison for fraud, conspiracy, and filing false documents. The scandal resulted in over 30,000 job cuts and over $180 billion in losses by investors.

American International Group (AIG)

American International Group (AIG) is a US multinational insurance firm with over 88 million customers across 130 countries. In 2005, CEO Hank Greenberg was found guilty of stock price manipulation. The SEC's investigation into

Greenberg revealed a massive accounting fraud of almost $4 billion.

It was found that the company had booked loans as revenue in its books and forced clients to use insurers with whom the company had pre-existing payoff agreements. The company had also asked stock traders to inflate the company's share price. AIG was forced to pay a $1.64 billion fine to the SEC. The company also paid $115 million to a pension fund in Louisiana and $725 million to three pension funds in Ohio.

Lehman Brothers Scandal (2008)

Lehman Brothers was a global financial services firm based out of New York City, New York. It was one of the largest investment banks in the United States. During the 2008 financial crisis, it was discovered that the company had hidden over $50 billion in loans. These loans had been disguised as sales using accounting loopholes.

According to an SEC investigation, the company had sold toxic assets to banks in the Cayman Islands on a short-term basis. It was understood that Lehman Brothers would buy back these assets. This gave the impression that the company had $50 billion more in cash and $50 billion less in toxic assets. In the aftermath of the scandal, Lehman Brothers went bankrupt.

Nissan & Renault Scandal

Prior to these US charges, Japanese authorities brought charges against both Ghosn and Kelly for similar alleged wrongdoings in December 2018. Ghosn's fall from grace saw him ousted as Nissan and Mitsubishi's chairman, he stepped down as CEO of Renault and he was swept from power at the Renault-Nissan-Mitsubishi Alliance. He's been charged with misreporting income to financial regulators in Japan and using company funds for personal expenses, among other wrongdoings.

Ghosn worked with Kelly to hide $90 million of compensation from the public. The two also worked to add more than $50 million of retirement allowance for Ghosn. In total, the extra compensation added up to $140 million, though the SEC said it was never paid out.

The report, submitted by Nissan to the Tokyo Stock Exchange on Thursday, details "personal expenses of Mr Ghosn" which it claimed were "unrelated to corporate purposes".

These include:

- Dinners at the Marmottan Museum in Paris.
- Guest entertainment at the Cannes Film Festival.
- Jewellery purchased at Cartier stores.

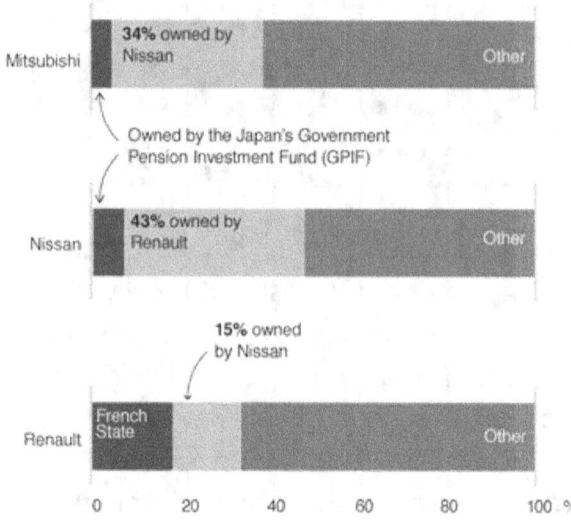

How the Alliance works
Size of stakes by car manufacturer

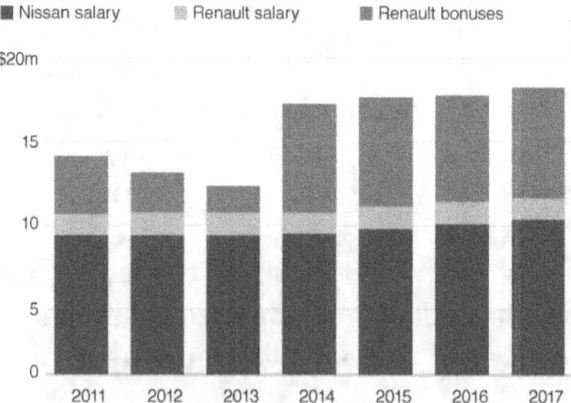

Ghosn's big pay
Official compensation

He is an internationally wanted fugitive. Ghosn has served as the CEO of Michelin North America, chairman and CEO of Renault, chairman of AvtoVAZ, chairman and CEO of Nissan, and chairman of Mitsubishi Motors. Ghosn was also chairman and CEO of the Renault–Nissan–Mitsubishi Alliance, a strategic partnership among those automotive manufacturers through a complex cross-shareholding agreement. The venture has held approximately 10% of the total market share since 2010, and as of 2017, was reckoned to be the largest automobile group worldwide.

On 30 December 2019, numerous media outlets reported that Ghosn had escaped from Japan and arrived in Beirut, Lebanon. Ghosn later confirmed these reports through a statement released by his press representative in New York. In his statement, Ghosn claimed that he would "no longer be held hostage by a rigged Japanese justice system where guilt is presumed, discrimination is rampant and basic human rights are denied."

It is unclear as to how Ghosn was able to leave Japan under the conditions of his bail. Japanese public broadcaster NHK quoted investigative sources who stated that Ghosn left his Tokyo apartment at around 14:30 on 29 December and joined two men at a nearby hotel. The three then took a bullet train from Shinagawa to Osaka and arrived at a hotel near Kansai International Airport just after 20:00. The team hired to extract him from Tokyo had noticed that Japanese security did not follow Ghosn into hotels, which facilitated his escape. A few hours later, two men left the hotel carrying large containers, including an audio equipment box where Ghosn was hidden. The men then boarded a Bombardier Global Express private jet with Turkish registration TC-TSR.

The large box carrying Ghosn was never x-rayed or checked by customs officials, because it was too big to fit inside the x-ray machine; the plane left Kansai Airport at 23:10, landing at Istanbul Atatürk Airport at 5:26 on the morning of 30 December. Within an hour of the plane's landing, a separate private jet left for Beirut. An employee at Turkish private jet operator MNG Jet admitted to falsifying passenger records, in which two separate planes were leased, one from Dubai to Osaka and then Osaka to Istanbul, while the other from Istanbul to Beirut.

Investor has lost 81% of their investment in Renault and Nissan.

Above all example state that when the investor, invest in such companies for the good return from the investment, but fails to understand the integrity of the management .In investing this kind of frauds happen and we as a value investor should not invest in this type of company that is the reason we should perform due diligence, understanding not only product for income statement, but as well as how is the management, board members, the CEO.

It is important for boards to manage governance because it creates efficiency in the work that they do. In addition, good governance practices highlight instances of errors and problems. By flagging potential issues, boards have the chance to respond quickly and appropriately. A focus on good governance holds the board accountable for improving efficiency, which also lends itself to reducing costs. When boards practice good governance, all processes run smoothly. There is less chance of crisis where the board needs to react rather than act and they have the proper time to be responsible in their acts and decision-making. Organizations that have a culture that supports good governance practices are more likely to offer quality products and services that meet the demands and expectations of the public.

Good governance lends assurance to shareholders and stakeholders that the organization is being transparent about their finances and conduct and that they're treating all people with dignity and respect. Best practices result from good governance and create a framework where all companies and organizations can measure themselves against.

Good governance assures us of many things including that it reduces risk and prevents fraud and unscrupulous behavior. When we put it all together, good governance leads to growth and success which is the whole reason for organizations to form in the first place.

Q&A

- Corporate governance?
- Your Answer

- What you have learned from Nissan & Renault Scandal?
- Your Answer

- We look for three things when we hire people. We look for intelligence, we look for initiative or energy, and we look for integrity. And if they don't have the latter, the first two will kill you?
- Your Answer

- If you were invested in Nissan & Renault stock and you got the news of unethical management, what you have done with your investment?
- Your Answer

9

Financial Distress

Many investor not look for quality income state and balance sheet and cash flow , they buy the stock only hope that the price will raise , and it never happen , if the company will do well , eventually it will reflect in the stock price , there is nothing a rocket science .Most of investor don't understand the basic principal of investing .

Investor invest in financial distress company, hope for the better tomorrow. Financial distress is a condition in which a company or individual cannot generate revenue or income because it is unable to meet or cannot pay its financial obligations. This is generally due to high fixed costs, illiquid assets, or revenues sensitive to economic downturns.

Ignoring the signs of financial distress can be devastating for a company. There may come a time when severe financial distress cannot be remedied because the company or individual's obligations are too high and cannot be paid, and there is just not enough revenue to offset the debt. If this happens, bankruptcy may be the only option.

If a company or individual experiences a period of time when it cannot pay its bills and other obligations by their due date, it is likely experiencing financial distress. Some of these expenses may include (expensive) financing, opportunity costs of projects, and employees who aren't productive. Employees of a distressed firm usually have lower morale and higher stress caused by the increased chance of bankruptcy, which could force them out of their jobs.

Companies under financial distress may find it difficult to secure financing. They may also find their market value dropping significantly, customers cutting back orders, and suppliers changing their terms of delivery.

Looking at a company's financial statement can help investors and others determine its financial health. For example, negative cash flow under the cash flow statements is one indicator of financial distress. This could be caused by a big difference between cash payments and receivables, high interest payments, and a drop in working capital.

Individuals who experience financial distress may find themselves in a situation where their debts are much more than their monthly income. This includes home or rent payments, car payments, and credit card and utility bills. People who experience situations like these tend to go through it for an extended period of time.

There are multiple warning signs to indicate a company is experiencing financial distress. Poor profits may indicate a company is financially unhealthy. Struggling to break even indicates a business cannot sustain itself from internal funds and needs to raise capital externally. This raises the company's business risk and lowers its creditworthiness with lenders, suppliers, investors, and banks. Limiting access to funds typically results in a company (or individual) failing.

Poor sales growth or decline indicates the market is not positively receiving a company's products or services based on its business model. When extreme marketing activities result in no growth, the market may not be satisfied with the offerings, and the company may close down. Likewise, if a company offers poor quality products or services, consumers start buying from competitors, eventually forcing a business to close its doors.

When debtors take too much time paying their debts to the company, cash flow may be severely stretched. The business or individual may be unable to pay its own liabilities. The risk is especially enhanced when a company has one or two major customers.

Do financial Analysis to understand company financial position.

Revenues

- Revenue growth (revenue this period - revenue last period) ÷ revenue last period.

- Client ÷ total revenue. If a single customer generates a high percentage of your revenues, you could face financial difficulty if that customer stops buying. No client should represent more than 10 percent of your total revenues.

- Revenue per employee (revenue ÷ average number of employees). This ratio measures your business's productivity. The higher the ratio, the better. Many highly successful companies achieve over $1 million in annual revenue per employee.

Profits

- Gross profit margin (revenues – cost of goods sold) ÷ revenues. A healthy gross profit margin allows you to absorb shocks to revenues or cost of goods sold without losing the ability to pay for ongoing expenses.

- Operating profit margin (revenues – cost of goods sold – operating expenses) ÷ revenues. Operating expenses don't include interest or taxes. This determines your company's ability to make a profit regardless of how you finance operations (debt or equity). The higher, the better.

- Net profit margin (revenues – cost of goods sold – operating expenses – all other expenses) ÷ revenues. This is what remains for reinvestment into your business and for distribution to owners in the form of dividends.

Operational Efficiency

- Accounts receivables turnover (net credit sales ÷ average accounts receivable). This measures how efficiently you manage the credit you extend to customers. A higher number means your company is managing credit well; a lower number is a warning sign you should improve how you collect from customers.

- Inventory turnover (cost of goods sold ÷ average inventory). This measures how efficiently you manage inventory. A higher number is a good sign; a lower number means you either aren't selling well or are producing too much for your current level of sales.

Capital Efficiency and Solvency

- Return on equity (net income ÷ shareholder's equity). This represents the return investors are generating from your business.

- Debt to equity (debt ÷ equity). The definitions of debt and equity can vary, but generally this indicates how much leverage you're using to operate. Leverage should not exceed what's reasonable for your business.

Liquidity

- Current ratio (current assets ÷ current liabilities). This measures your ability to pay off short-term obligations from cash and other current assets. A value less than 1 means your company doesn't have sufficient liquid resources to do this. A ratio above 2 is best.

- Interest coverage (earnings before interest and taxes ÷ interest expense). This measures your ability to pay interest expense from the cash you generate. A value less than 1.5 is cause for concern to lenders.

Look for a Successful Company

It is often debated whether a commonly perceived "good" company, as defined by characteristics such as competitive advantage, stable earnings, above-average management, and market leadership, is also a good company in which to invest. While these characteristics of a good company can point toward a good investment, this article will explain how to also evaluate the company's financial characteristics and how to know if a company is a good investment.

Earnings growth is usually described as a percentage, in periods like year-over-year, quarter-over-quarter, and month-over-month. The basic premise of earnings growth is that the current reported earnings should exceed the previously reported earnings.

Earnings stability is a measure of how consistently those earnings have been generated over time. Stable earnings growth typically occurs in industries where growth has a more predictable pattern.

Earnings can grow at a rate similar to revenue growth; this is usually referred to as top-line growth and is more obvious to the casual observer. Earnings can also grow because a company is cutting expenses to add to the bottom line. It is important to verify where the stability is coming from when comparing one company to another.

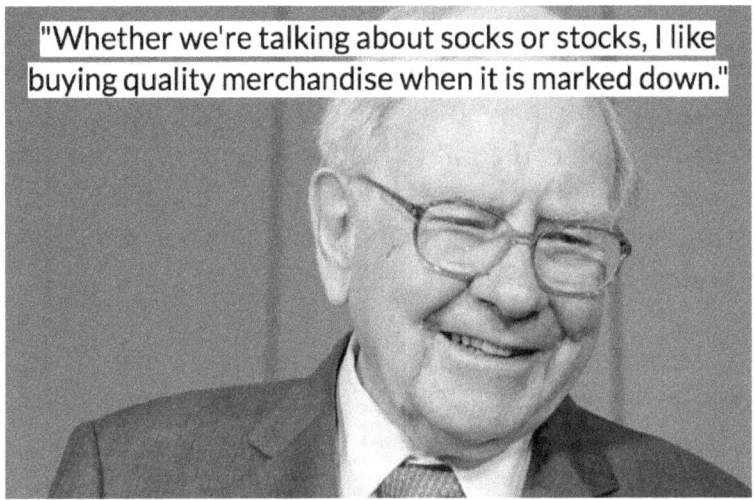

"Whether we're talking about socks or stocks, I like buying quality merchandise when it is marked down."

Berkshire's 1996 annual report:

"Companies such as Coca-Cola and Gillette might well be labeled "The Inevitables." Forecasters may differ a bit in their predictions of exactly how much soft drink or shaving-equipment business these companies will be doing in ten or twenty years...In the end, however, no sensible observer - not even these companies' most vigorous competitors, assuming they are assessing the matter honestly - questions that Coke and Gillette will dominate their fields worldwide for an investment lifetime.

Here's what Buffett had to say on that above-mentioned investor's question at the 1997 Berkshire annual meeting of shareholders:

"Because what I was doing in the annual report is I had talked about Coke and Gillette as being "The Inevitables," and what wonderful businesses they were.

And I thought it appropriate, particularly — the report goes to a lot of people — that they would not take that as an unqualified buy recommendation about the companies, because they're absolutely wonderful companies run by outstanding managers. But you can pay too much, at least in the short run, for businesses like that.

So I thought it was only appropriate to point out that no matter how wonderful a business it is, that there always is a risk that you will pay a price where it will take a few years for the business to catch up with the stock. That the stock can get ahead of the business.

But I didn't want particularly relatively unsophisticated people to see those names there and then think, "This guy is touting these as a wonderful buy."

Don't blindly invest, Buffett has tried to make it clear many times in the past that investors should always understand valuation first before they start investing, and not just follow tips blindly.

This advice is a continuation of that. If you don't understand how to value a business based on fundamentals and instead only buy stocks based on tips, you are destined to hit a speed bump at some point.

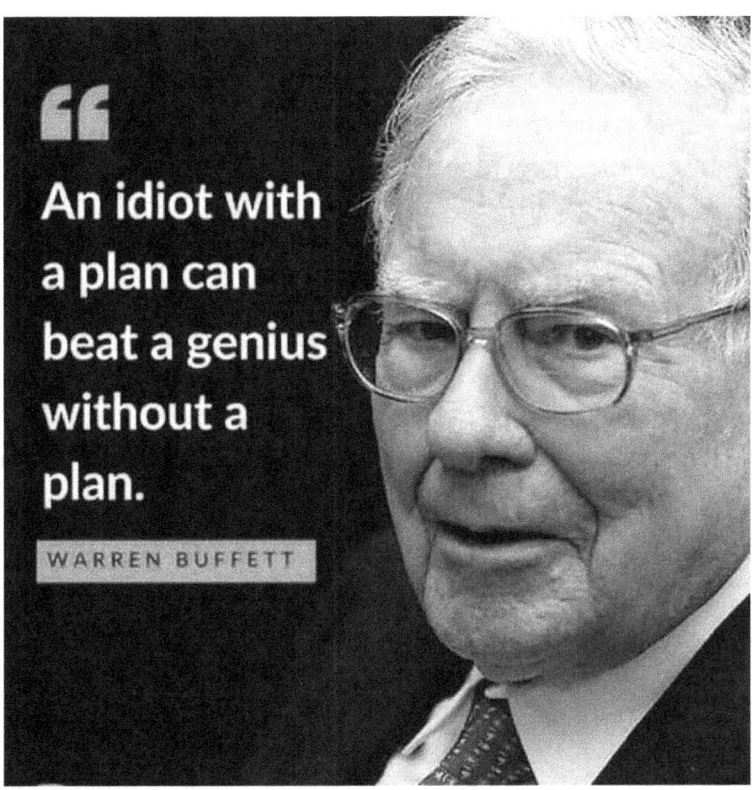

Quality investing is an investment strategy based on a set of clearly defined fundamental criteria that seeks to identify companies with outstanding quality characteristics. The quality assessment is made based on soft (e.g. management credibility) and hard criteria (e.g. balance sheet stability). Quality investing supports best overall rather than best-in-class approach.

The idea for quality investing originated in the bond and real estate investing, where both the quality and price of potential investments are determined by ratings and expert attestations. Later the concept was applied to investments in enterprises in equity markets.

Benjamin Graham, the founding father of value investing, was the first to recognize the quality problem among equities back in the 1930s. Graham classified stocks as either Quality or Low Quality. He also observed that the greatest losses result not from buying quality at an excessively high price, but from buying Low Quality at a price that seems good value. Warren Buffett said that one wants to buy companies that can be run by idiots, because some day they will be.

The quality issue in a corporate context attracted particular attention in the management economics literature following the development of the BCG matrix in 1970. Using the two specific dimensions of life cycle and the experience curve concept, the matrix allocates a company's products – and even companies themselves – to one of two quality classes (Cash Cows and Stars) or two Non-quality classes (Question Marks and Dogs). Other important works on quality of corporate business can be found primarily among the US management literature. These include, for example, "In Search of Excellence" by Thomas Peters and Robert Waterman, "Competitive Advantage" by Michael Porter, "Built to Last" by Jim Collins and Jerry Porras, and "Good to Great" by Jim Collins.

Quality investing gained credence in particular after the burst of the Dot-com bubble in 2001 when investors witnessed the spectacular failures of companies such as Enron and Worldcom. These corporate collapses focused investors' awareness on quality, which may vary from stock to stock. Investors started to pay more attention to quality of balance sheet, earnings quality, information transparency, and corporate governance quality.

Q&A

- If you buy stock in a hope price will raise, what will happen if there is a big market crash?
- Your Answer

- Investor invest in financial distress company, hope for the better tomorrow why?
- Your Answer

10

Valuation

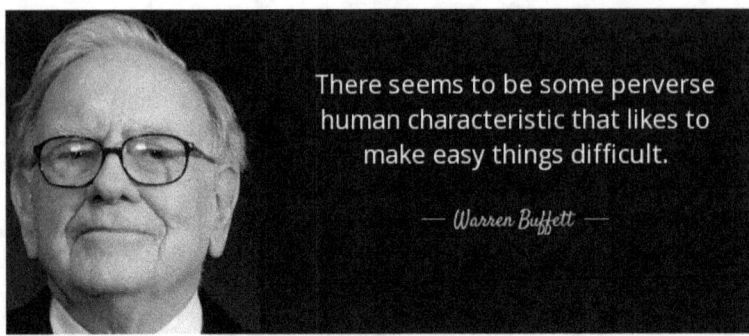

The Heart of Value Investing

Many investor do a valuation by using Discounted Cash Flow as what they have learn in the B school , but value investor , even warren buffet has never used DCF , you must be very surprised by now , what I am talking about , the truth is that , the value investor use Assets value (AV), Earning Power Value (EPV) and Franchise Value (FV), using this method value investor get the intrinsic value , you will be surprised again that value investor never predict cash flow , we value company as today's value , value investor are not a astrologer to predict any cash flow .

Value Investor never use two approaches

- Discounted Cash Flow
- EBIDTA

Every investor who wants to beat the market must master the skill of stock valuation. Essentially, stock valuation is a method of determining the intrinsic value (or theoretical value) of a stock. The importance of valuing stocks evolves from the fact that the intrinsic value of a stock is not attached to its current price. By knowing a stock's intrinsic value, an investor may determine whether the stock is over- or under-valued at its current market price.

Valuing stocks is an extremely complicated process that can be generally viewed as a combination of both art and science. Investors may be overwhelmed by the amount of available information that can be potentially used in valuing stocks.

Intrinsic value is a way of describing the perceived or true value of an asset. This is not always identical to the current market price because assets can be over- or undervalued. Intrinsic value is a common part of fundamental analysis, which investors use to assess stocks, as well being used in options pricing.

"Intrinsic value" is a philosophical concept, wherein the worth of an object or endeavor is derived in and of itself—or, in layman's terms, independent of other extraneous factors. A company's stock also is capable of holding intrinsic value, outside of what its perceived market price is, and is often touted as an important aspect to consider by value investors when picking a company to invest in.

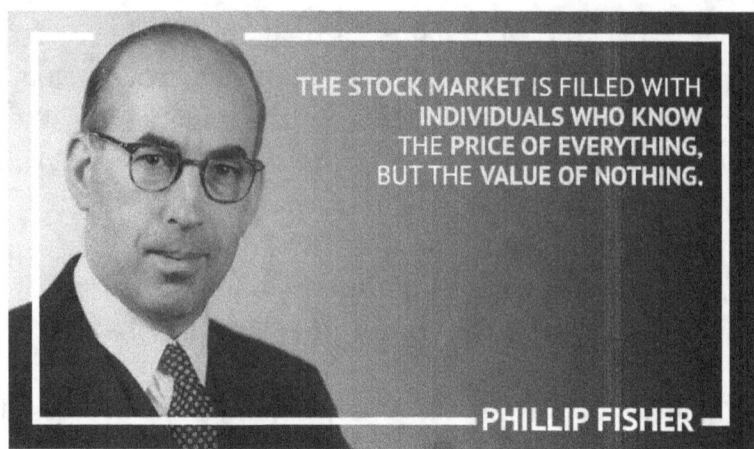

> THE STOCK MARKET IS FILLED WITH INDIVIDUALS WHO KNOW THE PRICE OF EVERYTHING, BUT THE VALUE OF NOTHING.
> — PHILLIP FISHER

The valuation method that is used by most value investors, analysts and fund managers to value assets is the Discount Cash Flow (DCF) method. Unlike the multiples method which is based on comparison with other companies, DCF valuation is based on the expected financial results of the company itself, thus it is the most reliable valuation method and gives the best estimate of the real value of the company.

Despite the fuzzy name, the main idea behind the DCF method is quite simple: each company is equal to the present value of all cash flows that are expected to be generated throughout its years of operation ('present value' means how much these cash flows are worth today. See further explanations below). To be complete, the cash and Equivalents on hand less the company total debt need to be added to the calculation. If the current stock price is lower than this fair value then the stock is considered cheap (undervalued), and if it is traded above this price it is expensive (overvalued).

DCF Valuation is extremely sensitive to assumptions related to perpetual growth rate and discount rate. Any minor tweaking here and there, and the DCF Valuation will fluctuate wildly and the fair value so generated won't be accurate.

It works best only when there is a high degree of confidence about future cash flows. But if the company's operations lack visibility, it becomes difficult to predict sales, operating expenses and capital investment with certainty. While forecasting cash flows for the next few years is difficult, pushing them out perpetually (mandatory for DCF Valuation) becomes almost impossible. As such, DCF method is susceptible to error if not properly accounted for these inputs.

No one can reliably predict how future innovations could impact the long-term viability of publicly traded firms.

- Requires a large number of assumptions.
- Prone to errors.
- Prone to overcomplexity.
- Very sensitive to changes in assumptions.
- A high level of detail may result in overconfidence.
- Looks at company valuation in isolation.
- Doesn't look at relative valuations of competitors.
- Terminal value is hard to estimate and represents a large portion of the total value.
- Challenging to estimate the Weighted Average Cost of Capital (WACC).

Buffett: "We don't formally have discount rates. Every time we start talking about this, Charlie reminds me that I've never prepared a spreadsheet, but I do in my mind. We just try to buy things that we'll earn more from than a government bond – the question is, how much higher?"

Munger: "Warren often talks about these discounted cash flows, but I've never seen him do one. If it isn't perfectly obvious that it's going to work out well if you do the calculation, then he tends to go on to the next idea."

Buffett: "It's true. If [the value of a company] doesn't just scream out at you, it's too close."

Munger: Some of the worst business decisions I've seen came with detailed analysis. The higher math was false precision. They do that in business schools, because they've got to do something.

Buffett: The priesthood has to look like they know more than "a bird in the hand." You won't get tenure if you say "a bird in the hand." False precision is totally crazy. The markets saw it in the Long-Term Capital Management [hedge fund] in 1998. It only happens to people with high IQs.

In Buffett's view, it is foolish to account for risk by fiddling with the discount rate. For one, it only makes sense to "deal with things about which we are quite certain." Buffett is only interested in opportunities where the probability of actually getting those future cash flows is as close to 100 percent as possible. In that case, it is appropriate to discount the cash flow using a risk-free rate.

Buffett: In a world of 7% long-term bond rates, we'd certainly want to think we were discounting the after-tax stream of cash at a rate of at least 10%. But that will depend on the certainty that we feel about the business. The more certain we feel about the business, the closer we're willing to play. We have to feel pretty certain about anything before we're even interested at all. But there are still degrees of certainty. If we thought we were getting a stream of cash over the thirty years that we felt extremely certain about, we'd use a discount rate that would be somewhat less than if it were one where we expected surprises or where we thought there were a greater possibility of surprises.

As Charlie Munger points out, it may not be easy to pin down intrinsic value. He says, "When you're trying to determine intrinsic value and margin of safety, there's no one easy method that can simply be mechanically applied by a computer that will make someone who pushes the buttons rich. You have to apply a lot of models. I don't think you can become a great investor rapidly, no more than you can become a bone-tumor pathologist quickly". (Berkshire Annual Meeting 2007).

Here is an easy explanation by Buffett of intrinsic value. Says Buffett, "Let's say you decide you want to buy a farm and you make calculations that you can make $70/acre as the owner. How much will you pay [per acre for that farm]? Do you assume agriculture will get better so you can increase yields? Do you assume prices will go up? You might decide you wanted a 7 per cent return, so you'd pay $1,000/acre. If it's for sale at $800, you buy, but if it's at $1,200, you don't." (Berkshire Annual Meeting 2007).

At best, intrinsic value is an estimate. "Intrinsic value is an estimate rather than a precise figure, and it is additionally an estimate that must be changed if interest rates move or forecasts of future cash flows are revised." You don't need to get intrinsic value figures right to the second decimal place. Buffett points out, "If we see someone who weighs 300 or 320 pounds, it doesn't matter - we know they're fat. We look for fat businesses." (Berkshire Annual Meeting 2007).

Warren Buffett shares some of his thoughts on EBITDA:

"It amazes me how widespread the use of EBITDA has become. People try to dress up financial statements with it."

"We won't buy into companies where someone's talking about EBITDA. If you look at all companies, and split them into companies that use EBITDA as a metric and those that don't, I suspect you'll find a lot more fraud in the former group. Look at companies like Wal-Mart, GE and Microsoft — they'll never use EBITDA in their annual report."

Value Investing Valuation Framework

The value of the assets

"We begin with the balance sheet and examine the value of the company's assets at the end of the most recent operating period, as determined by the company's accountants. We know that these accounting values are going to be more accurate for some assets than for others. Thus, as we work down the balance sheet, we accept or adjust the stated numbers as experience and analysis dictate.

Earnings power value

The second most reliable measure of a firm's intrinsic value is the second calculation made by Graham and Dodd, namely, the value of its current earnings, properly adjusted.

Market Value

The current market cap of the company.

If the Market Cap is less than the Earning Power Value, value investor buy the stock and have margin of safety.

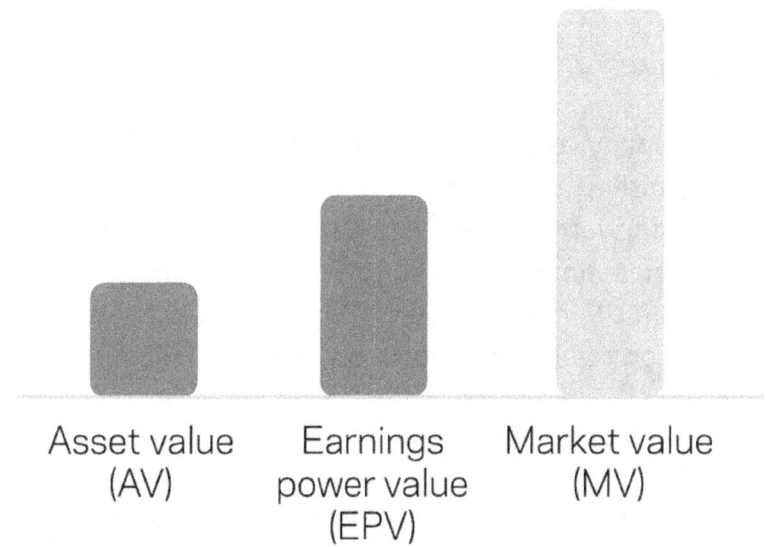

If EPV > MV buy the stock

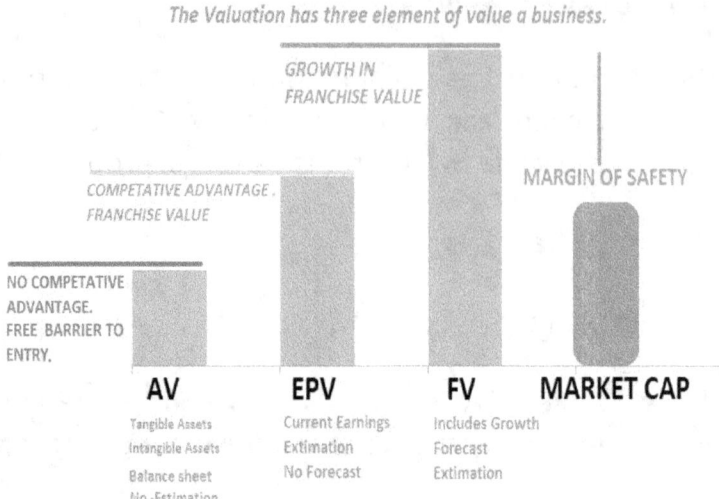

Franchise Value

If company create value to the shareholders and have competitive advantage and barrier to entry then we can move forward to calculate Franchise Value. Modern value investor estimate that company enjoy barrier to entry and they check franchise value, are company is having above return on equity and return on capital employed.

Always Invest with a Margin of Safety

Margin of safety is the principle of buying a security at a significant discount to its intrinsic value, which is thought to not only provide high-return opportunities but also to minimize the downside risk of an investment.

☐ In simple terms, Graham's goal was to buy assets worth $1 for 50 cents. He did this very, very well. To Graham, these business assets may have been valuable because of their stable earning power or simply because of their liquid cash value. For example, it wasn't uncommon for Graham to invest in stocks where the liquid assets on the balance sheet (net of all debt) were worth more than the total market cap of the company (also known as "net nets" to Graham followers). This means that Graham was effectively buying businesses for nothing. While he had a number of other strategies, this was the typical investment strategy for Graham.

This concept is very important for investors to note, as value investing can provide substantial profits once the market inevitably re-evaluates the stock and ups its price to fair value. It also provides protection on the downside if things don't work out as planned and the business falters. The safety net of buying an underlying business for much less than it is worth was the central theme of Graham's success. When chosen carefully, Graham found that a further decline in these undervalued **stocks occurred infrequently.**

Q&A

- The Heart of Value Investing is?
- Your Answer

- What DCF not tell?
- Your Answer

- Valuation approach by value investor?
- Your Answer

- Can you estimate free cash flow for a company after 10 year, what is the accuracy?

- Your Answer

- What are Assets Value, Earning Power Value and Market Value?
- Your Answer

- If the Market Cap is less than the Earning Power Value, value investor buy the stock and have margin of safety?
- Your Answer

11

Buffett FAQ

Have you ever bought a company where the numbers told you not to? How much is quantitative and how much is qualitative?

October 15th 1998

The best buys have been when the numbers almost tell you not to. Because then you feel so strongly about the product. And not just the fact you are getting a used cigar butt cheap. Then it is compelling. I owned a windmill company at one time. Windmills are cigar butts, believe me. I bought it very cheap, I bought it at a third of working capital. And we made money out of it, but there is no repetitive money to be made on it. There is a one-time profit in something like that. And it is just not the thing to be doing. I went through that phase. I bought streetcar companies and all kinds of things. In terms of the qualitative, I probably understand the qualitative the moment I get the phone call. Almost every business we have bought has taken five or ten minutes in terms of analysis. We bought two businesses this year.

General Re is an $18 billion deal. I have never been to their home office. I hope it is there. (Laughter) "There could be a few guys there saying what numbers should we send Buffett this month?" I could see them going once a month and saying we have $20 billion in the bank instead of $18 billion. I have never been there.

Before I bought Executive Jet, which is fractional ownership of jets, before I bought it, I had never been there. I bought my family a quarter interest in the program three years earlier. And I have seen the service and it seems to develop well. And I got the numbers. But if you don't know enough to know about the business instantly, you won't know enough in a month or in two months. You have to have sort of the background of understanding and knowing what you do or don't understand. That is the key. It is defining your circle of competence.

Everybody has got a different circle of competence. The important thing is not how big the circle is, the important thing is the size of the circle; the important thing is staying inside the circle. And if that circle only has 30 companies in it out of 1000s on the big board, as long as you know which 30 they are, you will be OK. And you should know those businesses well enough so you don't need to read lots of work. Now I did a lot of work in the earlier years just getting familiar with businesses and the way I would do that is use what Phil Fisher would call, the "Scuttlebutt Approach." I would go out and talk to customers, suppliers, and maybe ex-employees in some cases. Everybody. Everytime I was interested in an industry, say it was coal, I would go around and see every coal company. I would ask every CEO, "If you could only buy stock in one coal company that was not your own, which one would it be and why? You piece those things together, you learn about the business after awhile.

Funny, you get very similar answers as long as you ask about competitors. If you had a silver bullet and you could put it through the head of one competitor, which competitor and why? You will find who the best guy is in the industry. So there are a lot of things you can learn about a business. I have done that in the past on the business I felt I could understand so I don't have to do that anymore. The nice thing about investing is that you don't have to learn anything new. You can do it if you want to, but if you learn Wrigley's chewing gum forty years ago, you still understand Wrigley's chewing gum. There are not a lot of great insights to get of the sort as you go along. So you do get a database in your head.

I had a guy, Frank Rooney, who ran Melville for many years; his father-in-law died and had owned H.H. Brown, a shoe company. And he put it up with Goldman Sachs. But he was playing golf with a friend of mine here in Florida and he mentioned it to this friend, so my friend said "Why don't you call Warren?" He called me after the match and in five minutes I basically had a deal.

But I knew Frank, and I knew the business. I sort of knew the basic economics of the shoe business, so I could buy it. Quantitatively, I have to decide what the price is. But, you know, that is either yes or no. I don't fool a lot around with negotiations. If they name a price that makes sense to me, I buy it. If they don't, I was happy the day before, so I will be happy the day after without owning it.

What is your investment process?

Jan 2005

In the past some things were cheap enough WB could decide in a day (this was somewhat a function of a time period where companies would sell at 2-3x earnings)

Decisions should be obvious to onlookers. You should be able to explain why you bought something in a paragraph.

"I don't do DCF" (WB says he does a rough approximation in his mind)

Finding ideas is a function of cumulative knowledge over time. Something just comes along - usually an event takes place, like a good management team screwing up that creates the opportunity (WB seems to imply here that his reading isn't specifically targeted at finding ideas, but rather that ideas jump out at him as a natural consequence of vociferous reading)

You must be patient...good ideas tend to be clustered together, and may not come at even time intervals...when you don't find anything for a while it can be irritating

WB isn't bothered by missing something outside his circle of competence - Missing things inside the circle is nerve racking...examples include WMT, FNM.

How do you build your investment knowledge?

Year 2003

We read a lot: daily publications, annual reports, 10Ks, 10Qs, business magazines, etc.

Fortunately, the investment business is one where knowledge accumulates and builds into a knowledge base that's useful. There's a lot to absorb over time. 40-50 years ago, I visited a lot of companies, but haven't done this in a long, long time.

[CM: The more basic knowledge you have, the less new knowledge you have to get. The guy who plays chess blindfolded [a chess master comes to Omaha during Berkshire's annual meeting weekend and, in an exhibition, plays multiple players blindfolded] -- he has a knowledge of the board, which allows him to do this. I'd hate to give up The Wall Street Journal.]

You'd also hate to give up the Buffalo News [which Berkshire owns]. [Laughter.] You want to read a lot of financial publications. The New York Times has a much better business section than it had 25 years ago. Read Fortune.

I don't read any analyst reports. If I read one, it's because the funny pages weren't available. I don't know why anyone does it.

What advice would you give to new investors?

I think you should read everything you can. In my case, by the age of 10, I'd read every book in the Omaha public library about investing, some twice. You need to fill your mind with various competing thoughts and decide which make sense. Then you have to jump in the water – take a small amount of money and do it yourself. Investing on paper is like reading a romance novel vs. doing something else. [Laughter] You'll soon find out whether you like it. The earlier you start, the better.

At age 19, I read a book [The Intelligent Investor] and what I'm doing today, at age 76, is running things through the same thought process I learned from the book I read at 19.

I remain big on reading everything in sight. And when you get the opportunity to meet someone like Lorimer Davidson, as I did, jump at it. I probably learned more in that four hours than in almost any course in college or business school.

What filters do you use when looking at companies?

Time: May 1997

[CM: Well, opportunity cost is a huge filter in life. If you've got two suitors who are eager to have you, but one is way better than the other, you're going to choose that one rather than the other. That's the way we filter stock buying opportunities. Our ideas are so simple. People keep asking us for mysteries, but all we have are the most elementary ideas.]

We know instantly whether a business is something we're going to understand, and whether it's a business that's going to have a sustainable edge, and that gets rid of a very significant percentage of opportunities. I'm sure people regard me and Charlie as very arbitrary--in the middle of the first sentence, we'll say, "We appreciate the call, but we're not interested." I'm sure that if they explain something I might get buttered on it, but we really can tell in the middle of the first sentence whether those two factors exist ... We can sometimes tell by who we're dealing with, whether a deal is ever going to work out or not. I mean, if there's an auction going on, we have no interest in talking about it. If someone is interested in doing that with their business, then they're going to want to sit down and renegotiate everything with us all over again after the deal is done ...We don't want to listen to stories all day, and we don't need brokerage reports. There's other things to do with your time.

[CM: Another filter is the concept of the quality person, which most people define as someone very much like themselves. (laughter) There are so many wonderful people out there, and there are so many awful people out there. And there are signs, like flags, waving over the awful people. And generally speaking, those people are to be avoided.]

What's the temperament of successful investors?

Time: 2003

[CM: I think there's something to be said for developing the disposition to own stocks without fretting.]

I think it's almost impossible to do well investing over time without this. If the market closed for years, we wouldn't care. Would still keep making Sees candy, Dilly bars, etc.

If you focus on the price, you're assuming that the market knows more than you do. That may be the truth, but in that case you shouldn't own it. The stock market is there to serve you, not to instruct you.

Focus on price and value. If a stock gets cheaper and you have some cash, buy more. We sometimes stop buying when prices goes up. This cost us $8 billion a few years ago when we were buying Wal-Mart. When we're buying something, we want the price to go down and down and down.

You don't have to be right on everything or 20%, 10%, or 5% of businesses. You only have to be right one or two times a year. I used to handicap horses. You can come up with a very profitable decision on a single company. If someone asked me to handicap the 500 companies in the S&P 500, I wouldn't do a very good job. You only have to be right a few times in your lifetime, as long as you don't make any big mistakes.

[CM: What's funny is that most big investment organizations don't think like this. They hire lots of people, evaluate Merck vs. Pfizer and every stock in the S&P 500, and think they can beat the market. You can't do it. Very few people have adopted our approach.]

Ted Williams, in his book The Science of Hitting, talked about how he carved up the strike zone into different zones and only swung at pitches that were in his sweet spot. Investing is the same way.

Could you explain more about the circle of competence?

Time: 2006

We are best at evaluating businesses where we can come to a judgment that they will look a lot like they do now in five years. The businesses will change, but the fundamentals won't. Iscar will be better – maybe a lot bigger – in five years, but the fundamentals will be the same. [In contrast,] look at how much telecom has changed.

Charlie says we have three boxes: In, Out and Too Hard. You don't have to do everything well. At the Olympics, if you run the 100 meters well, you don't have to do the shot put.

Tom Watson [the founder of IBM] said, "I'm no genius. I'm smart in spots and I stay around those spots." We have a lot of managers who are the same. You don't want to compete with Pete Liegl [the CEO of Forest River, Inc.] because he'll kill you in the RV business. But he doesn't try to tell us how to run the insurance business.

I was virtually there at the birth of Intel. I was on the board of Grinnell College with Bob Noyce [one of the founders of Intel] and Grinnell invested $300,000 into it at inception. [I easily could have as well, but] I had no idea then and still don't now what Intel will look like in five years. Even people in the industry don't. Some businesses are very, very hard to predict.

[CM: A foreign correspondent, after talking to me for a while, once said: "You don't seem smart enough to be so good at what you're doing. Do you have an explanation?" [Laughter]]

Buffett: Was he referring to me or you? [Laughter]

[CM: I said, "We know the edge of our competency better than most." That's a very worthwhile thing. It's not a competency if you don't know the edge of it.]

Could you give us your definition of stock market risk?

Time: May 1997

We think first in terms of business risk. The key to Graham's approach to investing is not thinking of stocks as stocks or part of the stock market. Stocks are part of a business. People in this room own a piece of a business. If the business does well, they're going to do all right as long as long as they don't pay way too much to join in to that business. So we're thinking about business risk. Business risk can arise in various ways. It can arise from the capital structure. When somebody sticks a ton of debt into a business, if there's a hiccup in the business, then the lenders foreclose. It can come about by their nature--there are just certain businesses that are very risky. Back when there were more commercial aircraft manufacturers, Charlie and I would think of making a commercial airplane as a sort of bet-your-company risk because you would shell out hundreds and hundreds of millions of dollars before you really had customers, and then if you had a problem with the plane, the company could go. There are certain businesses that inherently, because of long lead time, because of heavy capital investment, basically have a lot of risk. Commodity businesses have a lot of risk unless you're a low-cost producer, because the low-cost producer can put you out of business. Our textile business was not the low-cost producer. We had fine management, everybody worked hard, we had cooperative unions, all kinds of things. But we weren't the low-cost producers so it was a risky business. The guy who could sell it cheaper than we could made it risky for us. We tend to go into businesses that are inherently low risk and are capitalized in a way that that low risk of the business is transformed into a low risk for the enterprise. The risk beyond that is that even though you identify such businesses, you pay too much for them. That risk is usually a risk of time rather than principal, unless you get into a really extravagant situation. Then the risk becomes the risk of you yourself--whether you can retain your belief in the real fundamentals of the business and not get too concerned about the stock market. The stock market is there to serve you and not to instruct you. That's a key to owning a good business and getting rid of the risk that would otherwise exist in the market.

You mention volatility--it doesn't make any difference to us whether the volatility of the stock market is a half a percentage of a point a day, or a quarter percent a day, or five percent a day. In fact, we'd probably make a lot more money if volatility was higher because it would create more mistakes in the market. Volatility is a huge plus to the real investor. Ben Graham used the example of Mr. Market. Ben said that just imagine that when you bought a stock you in effect bought into a business where you have this obliging partner who comes around every day and offers you a price at which he'll either buy or sell and that price is identical. No one ever gets that in a private business, where daily you get a buy-sell offer by a party. But you get that in the stock market, and that's a huge advantage. And it's a bigger advantage if this partner of yours is a heavy-drinking manic depressive. (laughter) The crazier he is, the more money you're going to make. So, as an investor, you love volatility. Not if you're on margin, but if you're an investor you're not on margin, and if you're an investor you love to get these wild swings because it means more things are going to get mispriced. Actually, volatility in recent years has dampened from what it used to be. It looks bigger because people think in terms of Dow points, but volatility was much higher many years ago than it is now. The amplitude of the swings used to be really wild and that gave you more opportunity. Charlie?

[CM: Well it came to be that corporate finance departments at universities developed the notion of risk-adjusted returns. My best advice to all of you would be to totally ignore this development. Risk had a very good colloquial meaning, meaning a substantial chance that something could go horribly wrong, and the finance professors sort of got volatility mixed up with a bunch of foolish mathematics and to me it's less rational than what we do. And I don't think we're going to change.]

Finance departments believe that volatility equals risk. They want to measure risk, and they don't know how to do it, basically. So they said volatility measures risk. I've often used the example of the Washington Post's stock. When I first bought it in 1973 it had gone down almost 50%, from a valuation of the whole company of close to $170 million down to $80 million. Because it happened pretty fast, the beta of the stock had actually increased, and a professor would have told you that the company was more risky if you bought it for $80 million than if you bought it for $170 million. That's something I've thought about ever since they told me that 25 years ago and I still haven't figured it out. (laughter)

What are your views on diversification?

Time: February 2008

I have 2 views on diversification. If you are a professional and have confidence, then I would advocate lots of concentration. For everyone else, if it's not your game, participate in total diversification. The economy will do fine over time. Make sure you don't buy at the wrong price or the wrong time. That's what most people should do, buy a cheap index fund, and slowly dollar cost average into it. If you try to be just a little bit smart, spending an hour a week investing, you're liable to be really dumb.

If it's your game, diversification doesn't make sense. It's crazy to put money into your 20th choice rather than your 1st choice. "Lebron James" analogy. If you have Lebron James on your team, don't take him out of the game just to make room for someone else. If you have a harem of 40 women, you never really get to know any of them well.

Charlie and I operated mostly with 5 positions. If I were running 50, 100, 200 million, I would have 80% in 5 positions, with 25% for the largest. In 1964 I found a position I was willing to go heavier into, up to 40%. I told investors they could pull their money out. None did. The position was American Express after the Salad Oil Scandal. In 1951 I put the bulk of my net worth into GEICO. Later in 1998, LTCM was in trouble. With the spread between the on-the-run versus off-the-run 30 year Treasury bonds, I would have been willing to put 75% of my portfolio into it. There were various times I would have gone up to 75%, even in the past few years. If it's your game and you really know your business, you can load up.

Over the past 50-60 years, Charlie and I have never permanently lost more than 2% of our personal worth on a position. We've suffered quotational loss, 50% movements. That's why you should never borrow money. We don't want to get into situations where anyone can pull the rug out from under our feet.

In stocks, it's the only place where when things go on sale, people get unhappy. If I like a business, then it makes sense to buy more at 20 than at 30. If McDonalds reduces the price of hamburgers, I think it's great.

What do you think of discounted cash flow (DCF) models?

Time: 2009

Buffett: All investing is laying out cash now to get some more back in the future. The concept of "a bird in the hand" came from Aesop in about 600 BC. He knew a lot, but not that [he lived in] 600 BC. He couldn't know everything. [laughter] The question is, how many birds are in the bush? What is the discount rate? How confident are you that you'll get [the bird]? Et cetera. That's what we do. If you need to use a computer or calculator to figure it out, you shouldn't [buy the investment]. Those types of [situations] fall into the "too-hard" bucket. It should be obvious. It should shout at you, without all the spreadsheets. We see something better.

Munger: Some of the worst business decisions I've seen came with detailed analysis. The higher math was false precision. They do that in business schools, because they've got to do something.

Buffett: The priesthood has to look like they know more than "a bird in the hand." You won't get tenure if you say "a bird in the hand." False precision is totally crazy. The markets saw it in the Long-Term Capital Management [hedge fund] in 1998. It only happens to people with high IQs. The markets of mid-September last year were [such that] you can't calculate standard deviations. People's actions don't observe laws of math. It's a terrible mistake to think higher math will take you a long way— you don't need to understand it, [and] it may lead you down the wrong path.

When did you know you were rich?

Time: May 6, 2005

I really knew I was rich when I had $10,000. I knew along time ago that I was going to be doing something I loved doing with people that I loved doing it with. In 1958, I had my dad take me out of the will, as I knew I would be rich anyway. I let my two sisters have all the estate.

I bet we all in this room live about the same. We eat about the same and sleep about the same. We pretty much drive a car for 10 years. All this stuff doesn't make it any different. I will watch the Super Bowl on a big screen television just like you. We are living the same life. I have two luxuries: I get to do what I want to do every day and I get to travel a lot faster than you.

You should do the job you love whether or not you are getting paid for it. Do the job you love. Know that the money will follow. I travel distances better than you do. The plane is nicer. But that is about the only thing that I do a whole lot different.

I didn't know my salary when I went to work for Graham until I got his first paycheck. Do what you love and don't even think about the money. I will take a trip on Paul Allen's Octopus ($400M yacht), but wouldn't want one for myself. A 60 man crew is needed. They could be stealing, sleeping with each other, etc. Professional sports teams are a hassle, especially when you have as much money as him. Fans would complain that you aren't spending enough when the team loses.

If there is a place that is warm in the winter and cool in the summer, and you do what you love doing, you will do fine. You're rich if you are working around people you like. You will make money if you are energetic and intelligent. This society lets smart people with drive earn a very good living. You will be no exception.

What makes a great business?

Time: 2005

The best businesses can maintain their earnings without continued reinvestment, whereas in the worst you have to keep pouring money into a money-losing business.

The best business is being the best surgeon in town. You don't have to do any reinvestment – the investment was the education. The surgeon will retain his earnings power, regardless of inflation.

[Untapped pricing power. The measure of a great business.]

We like buying businesses with some untapped pricing power. For example, when we bought See's for $25 million, I asked myself, "If we raised prices by 10 cents per pound, would sales fall off a cliff?" The answer was obviously no. You can determine the strength of a business over time by the amount of agony they go through in raising prices.

A good example is newspapers. The local daily paper controlled the market and every year they raised the [advertising] rates and circulation prices – it was almost a big yawn. They didn't worry about losing big advertisers like Sears, JC Penney or Wal-Mart, or losing subscribers. They increased prices whether the price of newsprint went up or down.

Now, they agonize over price increases because they worry about driving people to other mediums. That world has changed.

You can learn a lot about the durable economics of a business by watching price behavior. The beer industry is able to raise prices, but it's getting tougher.

When you are looking at a business in which to invest, what are your priorities?

Time: 2001

You have to really understand the economics of a business and the kind of people you are getting into business with. They have to love their business. They have to feel that they have been creative, that it is their painting, I am not going to disturb it, just give them more canvas and more brushes, but its their painting, from our standpoint any way. The whole place will reflect the attitude of the person at the top, if you have someone at the top who doesn't care, the people down below won't care. On the other hand, if you have someone at the top who cares a great deal, that will be evident across the organization. [The type of people managing the business is a very important criteria, then?] Yes, contracts don't protect you; you have to have confidence in the people.

What do you think the best quality is in a business or a person?

Time: 2010

There are many important qualities to have in a business and many important qualities in a person. In a business always look for a great product at a fair price, and with honest reliable management. In a person, I think that honesty, brains, and hard work are very important qualities. People who demonstrate these consistently, will usually be successful in whatever they do.

Do you invest based on trends or sectors?

Time: 2006

We don't play big trends like demographic trends. They just don't mean that much. There's too much money to be made year to year than worry about trends that take ten years to play out. I can't think of one investment we've ever made based on a macro or demographic trend.

[CM: Not only that, but we've missed the biggest commodity boom in history – and we'll continue to miss things like this!]

But we'll search for new ways to fail! [Laughter]

What is your analysis of Coca-Cola?

Time: October 15th 1998

Well, basically I love it, but because the market for Coca-Cola products will grow far faster over the next twenty years internationally than it will in the United States. It will grow in the U.S. on a per capita basis. The fact that it will be a tough period for who knows—three months or three years—but it won't be tough for twenty years. People will still be going to be working productively around the world and they are going to find this is a bargain product in terms of a portion of their working day that they have to give up in order to have one of these, better yet, five of them a day like I do.

This is a product that in 1936 when I first bought 6 of those for a quarter and sold them for a nickel each. It was in a 6.5 oz bottle and you paid a two cents deposit on the bottle. That was a 6.5 oz. bottle for a nickel at that time; it is now a 12 oz. can which if you buy it on Weekends or if you buy it in bigger quantities, so much money doesn't go to packaging—you essentially can buy the 12 ozs. for not much more than 20 cents. So you are paying not much more than twice the per oz. price of 1936. This is a product that has gotten cheaper and cheaper relative to people's earning power over the years. And which people love. And in 200 countries, you have the per capita consumption use going up every year for a product that is over 100 years old that dominates the market. That is unbelievable.

One thing that people don't understand is one thing that makes this product worth 10s and 10s of billions of dollars is one simple fact about really all colas, but we will call it Coca-Cola for the moment. It happens to be a name that I like. Cola has no taste memory. You can drink one of these at 9 O'clock, 10 O'clock, 1 O'clock and 5 O'clock. The one at 5 o'clock will taste as good to you as the one you drank early in the morning, you can't do that with Cream Soda, Root Beer, Orange, Grape. All of those things accumulate on you. Most foods and beverages accumulate; you get sick of them after a while. And if you eat See's Candy—we get these people who go to work for us at See's Candy and the first day they go crazy, but after a week they are eating the same amount as if they were buying it, because chocolate accumulates on you. There is no taste memory to Cola and that means you get people around the world who will be heavy users—who will drink five a day, or for Diet Coke, 7 or even 8 a day. They will never do that with other products. So you get this incredible per capita consumption. The average person in this part of the world or maybe a little north of here drinks 64 ozs. of liquid a day. You can have 64 ozs. of that be Coke and you will not get fed up with Coke if you like it to start with in the least. But if you do that with anything else; if you eat just one product all day, you will get a little sick of it after a while.

It is a huge factor. So today over 1 billion of Coca-Cola product servings will be sold in the world and that will grow year by year. It will grow in every country virtually, and it will grow on a per capita basis. And twenty years from now it will grow a lot faster internationally than in the U.S., so I really like that market better, because there is more growth there over time. But it will hurt them in the short term right now, but that doesn't mean anything. Coca-Cola went public in 1919; the stock sold for $40 per share. The Chandler family bought the whole business for $2,000 back in the late 1880s. So now he goes public in 1919, $40 per share. One year later it is selling for $19 per share. It has gone down 50% in one year. You might think it is some kind of disaster and you might think sugar prices increased and the bottlers were rebellious. And a whole bunch of things. You can always find reasons that weren't the ideal moment to buy it. Years later you would have seen the Great Depression, WW II and sugar rationing and thermonuclear weapons and the whole thing—there is always a reason.

But in the end if you had bought one share at $40 per share and reinvested the dividends, it would be worth $5 million now ($40 compounding at 14.63% for 86 years!). That factor so overrides anything else. If you are right about the business you will make a lot of money. The timing part of it is very tricky thing so I don't worry about any given event if I got a wonderful business what it does next year or something of the sort. Price controls have been in this country at various times and that has fouled up even the best of businesses. I wouldn't be able to raise prices Dec31st on See's Candy. But that doesn't make it a lousy business if that happens to happen, because you are not going to have price controls forever. We had price controls in the early 70s.

The wonderful business—you can figure what will happen, you can't figure out when it will happen. You don't want to focus too much on when but you want to focus on what. If you are right about what, you don't have to worry about when very much.

Would you buy McDonald's and go away for twenty years?

Time: October 15th 1998

McDonald's has a lot of things going for it, particularly abroad again. The position abroad in many countries is stronger than it is here. It is a tougher business over time. People don't want to be eating--exception to the kids when they are giving away beanie babies or something--at McDonald's every day. If people drink five Cokes a day, they probably will drink five of them tomorrow. The fast food business is tougher than that but if you had to pick one hand to have in the fast food business, which is going to be a huge business worldwide, you would pick McDonald's. I mean it has the strongest position.

It doesn't win taste test with adults. It does very well with children and it does fine with adults, but it is not like it is a clear winner. And it is gotten into the game in recent years of being more price promotional--you remember the experiment a year ago or so. It has gotten more dependent on that rather than selling the product by itself. I like the product by itself. I feel better about Gillette if people buy the Mach 3 because they like the Mach 3 than if they get a Beanie Baby with it. So I think fundamentally it is a stronger product if that is the case. And that is probably the case.

We own a lot of Gillette and you can sleep pretty well at night if you think of a couple billion men with their hair growing on their faces. It is growing all night while you sleep. Women have two legs, it is even better. So it beats counting sheep. And those are the kinds of business...(you look for). But what type of promotion am I going to put out there against Burger King next month or what if they sign up Disney and I don't get Disney? I like the products that stand alone absent price promotion or appeals although you can build a very good business based on that. And McDonald's is a terrific business. It is not as good a business as Coke. There really hardly are any. It is a very good business and if you bet on one company in that field bet on (garbled) McDonald's. We bought Dairy Queen a while back that is why I am plugging it shamelessly here.

What do you tell your managers at Berkshire?

Time: November 12th 2009

I send one message out every year and a half or two years. They get one letter from me every couple of years. And basically it says, run this business like it's the only business that your family can own for the next 100 years. You can't sell it. But every year don't measure it by the earnings in the quarter that year. Measure it by whether the moat around that business, what gives it competitive advantage over time has widened or narrowed. If you keep doing that for 100 years, it's going to work out very well. Then I tell them basically if the reason for doing something is everybody else is doing it, it's not good enough. If you have to use that as a reason, forget it. You don't have a good reason for doing something. Never use that.

www.ingramcontent.com/pod-product-compliance
Lightning Source LLC
Chambersburg PA
CBHW071358210526
45465CB00001B/150